Contents

Vol 94 No 3 Autumn

Poems

Essay

Reviews

Poet in the Gallery

Art

Poems

Fred Voss

HAMMERS AND HEARTS OF THE GODS

Best is the morning
when our hearts pound and our sugar spoons
ring TING TING TING TING TING
against the insides of our coffee mugs stirring
the strong black coffee as
a hundred machine motors fire up and we feel
as if we can hear
the feet of ants
tapping
across mountain rocks as our hands
grip machine handles and oil
and coolant begin to flow
across machine beds and we rowed
with Ulysses
through the smashing-together rocks past the singing sirens
toward home we
built
the Brooklyn Bridge drove the spikes down through the rails that spanned
a continent held
the ice
at the South Pole in our fist balanced
the ballerina
in the palm of our hand at Carnegie Hall thought
of the wheel
that opened the world best
is the morning
at 7:05 or 7:32 am as the oranges ripen on branches
tigers
roar at rising suns babies
take their first steps newspapers
slap down onto pavements locomotives
warm their engines

ready to cross mountains best
is the blood
still flowing through our veins the sea
still full of life the galaxies
still hanging
impossibly in the blackness as we lift our hammers
our wrenches
our hearts
our spirits
in this factory where the universe
was made.

FIELD OF POEMS

I am the only white man who works here
others
last a week or 2 and talk of knives
in tires
acid
in soap sure
those Mexicans who keep saying "Camerero" to them are out to get them
They fume
about their wages being driven down by all the illegal
alien Mexicans in this city
of L.A.
and then quit
leaving me alone with all these Mexicans again
alone
like I have always been
unable to speak
with this wrench in my hand
next to carved steel
and streets
where bullets fly and men sit in gutters looking up at the sky
holding wine bottles
full of better worlds
I like it here
in downtown L.A. where I am the only white man
I like it that all the other white men quit
or come for the interview and drive around the block a couple of times
and won't even set foot
inside these brick walls
At lunch the Mexicans pull out their guitars
or lie on their backs on cardboard sheets out in the gravel parking lot
and dream
as I smile
in this field
of poems.

Lucie McKee

TRAVEL

How quickly a voyage becomes a photograph –
there on my desk like a lost relative, familiar
though stilled, passed on to the other side,
but in this case arrested in its own native
landscape. What's vanished is the imaginary
world between home and a place so foreign
I collected a nest in my mind from both.
Even in the US once I was lost between North
and South, so much enthralled I didn't know
the way home, and southern pleasances had
forgotten all about me in the bustle of cars and
commerce. I have been ravished by gods of place
so many times I am the original mixed breed,
every region I have seen grafted on my skin like
one of those apple trees bearing every variety,
but my dreams now are as alien gases hovering
the haunted swamp I glide through at night.

THE ROAD MENDERS

Filming the drum of tar
boiling by the roadside on
a bright, orange fire
surrounded by stylish men,
women and children wearing
blue, yellow, red, green clothes
framing bronze faces:
high cheekbones,
eyes black as tar – I drive on,
white in white clothes,
forearm at ease along
the Jeep window, closed now
to road dust, black smoke,
car exhaust. People
pour molten tar from buckets
onto hand crushed rock
filling holes in the cliff-clasping
one lane mountain road.
Too hot, I guess, for shoes,
or gloves, or masks.
Nobody is fat. They are so
beautiful, I think this must be
a fitness class. Yes,
Thursday's hour to stretch
backs, shrink abdomens, tread
miles in place, keep up
a tan under an oracular sun
foretells no change
in the weather, no change
on this road at all.

Darjeeling – 2000 AD

Paul Batchelor

LEBIYSKA MOVA

He tells of *Kobzari*
      making their rounds
   at fairs & markets –
      blind street-singers
      keepers of a secret history
        the struggle
          for the Black Sea steppe
       Cossack rebellions
         fallen heroes
     the cruelty of the Turk –

Of impeccably played bandura
     & Fedir the Cold One
      sleeping in a ditch –
   Fedir with a voice
      like a jet of blood with grief in it
     proclaiming the truth
        in *lebiyska mova*
        a gospel in tomorrow's language –

Of a village where the butcher starves
   the shoemaker goes barefoot
   & someone saws a bed in half
    to make a bed

Died, all, in the terror

In a Mission
in Colonia Esperanca
     he composes
   a final *dumy*
     explaining
       to the anthropologist
       with his reel-to-reel
    that when the pitch is bent
     & sharp or flat notes
      slip into the scale
   it is called
      dodavaty zhaloshchiv:
   'adding the sorrow'

Anne-Marie Fyfe
RETREAT

The dacha tilts incautiously these days, the gash
more raw than before. Myopic
windows gaze on the morning's jet-stream.

Suitcases of tinsel and lights slither to attic-eaves.
A dismantled cot slumps against mattresses
as dresser crockery huddles to starboard.

Cars slow fender-tight, occupants meet
on fissured clay to examine impacted roots,
torn play-den clutter exposed, embarrassed . . .

A chimney-cowl crashes on the patio, red
earth tiles follow. South-facing shutters dangle
fearful, indolent towards an emptying fishpond.

DUE NORTH

Neighbours come to expect
her obdurate sculling at balcony windows
on the angle of Eglantine.
                              Rapt
in matty Peruvian coats, face
lifted north-easterly to the fall-out
of memorial light, perpetually
bowing to the skiff's prow,
paintered frettingly to rusting pipes.

As amber signals catch fire
she implores lone street-lamps
amid torrents, needles of glass darting.

With luck she will stall long enough
in the near sea-lane for a courtly
passer to embark; tilt the lodestone
plumb in his true palm; free
cold anxious oars from her fingers.

Helen Macdonald

TAXONOMY

Wren. Full song. No subsong. Call of alarm, spreketh & ought
damage the eyes with its form, small body, tail pricked up & beak like a hair

trailed through briars & at a distance scored with lime scent in the nose
like scrapings from a goldsmith's cuttle, rock alum & fair butter well-temped

which script goes is unrecognised by this one, is pulled by the ear
in anger the line at fault is under and inwardly drear as a bridge in winter

reared up inotherwise to seal the eyes through darkness, the bridge speaks
it does not speak, the starlings speak that steal the speech of men, *uc antea*

a spark that meets the idea of itself, apparently fearless.
Ah cruelty. And I had not stopped to think upon it

& I had not extended it into the world for love for naught.

POEM

Take a voice you know only
spliced, known as Pantagruel
and shut in a clasp of warm rose.
An elegiac feathering of black
singes the wood and imagines
a ludic impasse, I mean to
nothing you meant. And two
distances to demonstrate
an oratorial distress, by sight
who you might not ever calm
or comb out of mind, *might*,
leaning a little heavy on
suchlike benevolence pressing
a keel to my hand
and all the weather
prating it, yours as a gift.
I am in England.
There are rings on my brow.
      This is a friend.
That is a show of fire pinned
to the lapel's politic dart siring
the one with the ivory face, some
downy conjunction spun into blue, this is
too too a friend, whose open word carries
the land away, the heart flying strongly
to sea.

PARALLAX NONPAREIL

How did Newton, his 1676 discovery, aid our perception of colour?
Shall we apply his own theoria to a bunch of several lines
two bridges over the English Countryside involving moons
a little rushing water & a biddable theme: means to live
sweet as a die, & die sweetly into 10-space: how many
shadows there, on that shape? For a basic education?

There must be a place for EACH.
& if integrity softens, reckons itself
to be DEFT, kindness in parallel
then revenge is sweet. But being asked [at length]
to ALTER; as if whatever magnificent traffic
intends from its period stance a light, the cast
parries fashionable cuffs with an amiable use of those terms
qua love, call the stave's cause my rejection.

Nowhere near the gentle westerly slope
is listing the recent case a dream for consideration
of sorrow and origins, mistaking the gait for home.

THE NEW WORLD

Memetics are mute phylogenies and smarting.
What is a hand for but to be held? It is raining

in Georgia it is raining all over the world
applause rattles from the pilot's beak in choppy

breves & *savoir faire* lost somewhere between here
and home where the heart is whatever. The light

is hard in departures & tightness of the chest harder
weak toxicologies the accents of the dreams aren't murder

scene after scene ships demeanour with trade
sets a leaving tear on each cheek & fades

and says: this is a real blade, fifteenth century, Japan.
Or: a peculiarly Germanic form of armour, no holes for eyes

black all over, annealed, the frayed corporeal manner
as the mouth sups grounds, faults and folds the arms under

but the shade of your eyes approximates the blade's blued dorsal edge
indigent as the model's side or even air, seen from below

every moment describes some other music
and I cannot remember banality ever existing

These poems are taken from Helen Macdonald's *Shaler's Fish,* available from Etruscan Books, 28 Fowlers Court, Fore Street, Buckfastleigh, South Devonshire TQ11 0AA. www.seaham.i12.com/etruscan

Jeremy Over

MOUSTACHIOED

Seventy years later and we are still just a vaguely connected
series of squiggles sitting in the California sun,
eating our brown bag lunches in Monterey one day
and El Paso the next.

But this is definitely someone.
This is someone's dark-haired wife
looking down from her open window
to the public fountains in the square below.
She is waiting for something – perhaps for that moment
when the bloodstained six inch iron needles are finally lifted
and basketwork becomes music.

Or perhaps something else. In any event Mrs Williams
– for it is indeed she – is falling asleep now and dreaming
her way into an underwater cartoon adventure.
First she mimics the sounds of a passing turtle,
then a whale, a school of silvery fishes,
a jew's harp, various insects, sirens,
footsteps, fireworks, whaps, slaps
and finally an amoeba spreading
discretely under the lens of a microscope.

Notice the detail, complete down
to the Christmas lights on the shrubbery.
Note too how light from the front door window
spills on to the little front step, underscored
by a quick romping passage on the piano
before the rogue elephant of the orchestra
effs and blinds his way through a sweaty tango;
a springboard of sorts into a steaming bowl of soup
and some rather difficult questions.

Why is it that white and yellow
flowers are the first to appear in Spring?
And who do you suppose it was
planted those little seeds of envy in the first place?

I asked David that 'good fer'nuthin cheap fur coat'.
'What is all this? Is it really one of those cinematic sea-changes
as described by historians in Chesapeake Bay?
Or is it simply a case of dropping
Martini glasses, one by one, off the edge of the sideboard?'

His hand reached into the bedroom
and rifled through the books with diabolical glee
searching for all the rhythms and symbology, the whole caboodle
and a climactic scurry across the banquet table
towards a mouthwatering tower of cheesecake.

And beyond that, perhaps, to some quieter days
where we might go out to the backlot lake
and engage in a spot of illegal carp fishing.

DELIGHT IN   ORDER

Erased Herrick

(i)
  sweet
Kindles in

          crimson
       neglect
      do   confuse

  the
      shoes

             .

(ii)
A wee
                    wanton

               tract

     all   stomach
  cuff   and
       flow

Do more bewitch me than   hen art
              .

(iii)
A
          clot   on
A lawn

                      here and there

A   ning a   ving

A careless   hose

Do   itch me   art
  too   part.

(iv)
                  dress
    in

   fine
    lace
       son
      and

    wave

     string

  more   than
     ever .

Joanne Limburg

APART

He feels he is coming apart;
he screams all thought apart.

New mothers cradle their smiles,
every one playing a part.

A hardening drift of skin
marks the first pulling-apart.

In curtained portions of night,
the women were set apart.

One figure draws us together;
the next one whirls us apart.

What's that I see in his face?
My own face coming apart.

WATER

Under my ribs, a tank full of water;
the jerk of a limb makes waves in the water.

I watched the waves from the ferry's deck,
a terrible strength in the heave of the water.

As you come into land at JFK,
the world dissolves into light and water.

The end of grief is a loosening grip,
permitting the loved one to slip under water.

Taut as an angler intent on his line,
I wait to haul my child from the water.

Brian Henry

ANAESTHESIA

As if drowning occurs only at the shore, I drop
to a knee, ease my self onto one side, to thrash.

My love has done this to me and no one can care,
for to care would be to allow, and there is no one

to allow here. The ones here do not care to allow.

I see a bridge; it gathers me and the water, makes
my self a bank for the river. The bridge knows

how to gather, to make a bank of nothing,
which I am. Come to me, watch it work.

SEVERANCE PAY

Let's say it was a splinter, for the sake of.
And this splinter was a metaphor for the wound-
inflicting data collecting behind your sinus
passages, waxing in pools every night before
sleep strikes its own pithy chords. *Thwip. Thwip*
thwip. And this splinter will not kill you
though its resilience raises the question
of how long *you* can last before you begin
to take yourself too seriously. The ceiling fan
on its lowest setting, the air barely moves
through the room, barely cuts the light
from the streetlamp as your daughter kicks you,
a heel against your kidney twice quickly,
before you can twist out of reach closer to the edge
of the bed you used to own. You find it easy to forget
and this blooms into its own source – of regret,
of sustenance – as, now, two and a half days later,
your daughter, that much older than when this began,
kisses you in her sleep on the back of the head.

BAD APPLE

[day 1]

In this poem the sippy cup discovered under the table,
congealed milk inside it, will emerge as a symbol
of a souring relationship, left alone until it decays
and only then doused with soap and hot water, quick fix
that hides the smell of the germs but lets them live
and make the child sick to the stomach a day later.

[day 2]

When the father thinks of his life, it's always Later,
despite the Now being there, he at the table
forgetting why, exactly, he continues to live
where he has become not a person but a symbol
of what he, until now, despised too much to fix,
and he wonders what else he will lose as he decays.

[day 3]

The sestina is a horrid form, it drags as it decays,
feigning movement, Now yawning into Later,
as if teleutons were enough to redeem, or even fix,
the structure, a mess of a tower – chairs on a table –
or the lack of substance despite the symbol
that sneezes itself into the poem: *to live, to live.*

[day 4]

Pointedly reminded by a friend that he has much to live
and be thankful for, he thinks that which decays
is already worse than dead, for it is a symbol
with no power except what it promises for later –
a burst of light that comes when one is drunk, at a table,
spine garbled by this life, too fucked up to fix.

[*day 5*]

This stanza-a-day sestina, too messed up to fix,
expects a lot of one with other ways to live,
(mow, clip, wash, shine, sweep), table or no table,
form or no form, and jerks itself off as it decays
into middling pools of amnesia, saved for later
but forgotten immediately, symbol or no symbol.

[*day 6*]

What in the end is not an idea but a symbol
wrecks the poem beyond any possible fix
despite the wish to save each step for later
and think that to write is the same as to live,
and here, it is safe to say, the sestina decays,
sublimates like the dirt that rings the table.

[*day 7*]

That which decays does not, cannot live;
that which is a symbol will not fix
that which is held for later, putrid under the table.

TORNADO / WARNING

The day, that open sore, refusing to heal into night,
we hole up in the corner of the cellar, a pit of clay
tilting up at each side.
                   The water heater awake despite
the absence of bodies in the house (there is no need)
it builds, then boils, and the air around slides toward itself
/ as if the air has self / and dips below the floor above (nails
dangling) to sweep us from where we're crouched, afraid
the house will lift and spin across the sky like metal
wagon wheels breaking in the sidewalk.
                            Water cooks, would pool
if.
    You weep into my hands at the wind's first rush.
                              We feel
the pull from without, the slip in pressure that precedes the fall.
See the drop descend to hang then rise, to rescind, return.
The water will rust, the clay, the red, will swallow us
as the windows withdraw and the rafters (but not the nails) burn.

Justin Quinn

THREE PRAGUE ELEGIES

I

Snow comes swirling in across the plain.
The river slows then stalls with icy splinters
that lock its waters to the land. The window
was locked weeks back & small flaws in its pane

send exaggerations through the cold terrain:
the houses waver, branches are suddenly printed
in black letter, hills ripple slightly. This winter
there is no limit to the price of grain.

Odd glints of black, a flurry, a spreading blot,
then swarming from the line of the horizon
come seventy thousand men with sword & blazon.

They are marching on the city that forgot
its proper place & thought that it could tamper
with God's law in the Holy Roman Empire.

II

They flow like molten rock, their flesh & bone
engaged in grand manœuvres through the landscape
with millions of small adjustments & quick answers
to every contour, before they turn to stone

as Victory on a plinth, high & alone
except for the other allegorical stances
arranged in lines about the park, advancing
& retreating, solid but still flown

as much as these large snowflakes that descend
out of the soft grey spaces of the heavens,
out of treaty, reparation, settled grievance

(the villages of both enemy & friend
torched, their people sprawling in the loam),
& light upon a still extended limb.

III

The citizens lie in the waving grass
abandoned here & there. All round, the humming
of heavy insects on the wing. High summer
& the heat stands like thicknesses of glass.

The couples shift & move as slowly as
flies through honey. Each sweet ache is a summons
for unimaginable faces, the strangers coming
to share the day, as these young lovers pass

& stream off from here through the centuries
in both directions from this burning hour
of noon. Today the sun will climb no higher

& they'll mix with the shadows of the trees
as evening takes the city, & their sighing
will segue to the bickering of bird-song.

Andrea Brady

BUILDING SITE

It was easier for the mouth than laughing better
exercise for the temporarium,
though planks got stuck and exhaled drafts
and soaped now, with the unbuttoning of your skin.
So your fingers slip out of gloves as the leads'
bodies drop into the city crevasse – their joy cannot be
imagined as they pass floors 30 to 40.   Not put out
by the cone, we would not be put out by the blinding
light. Shines a filament of pure silver nerve from each
currier queuing in front of the forge. They're gorgeous,
kind of social, gone wild with follies. Badged and in blue
wigs, agents of desire slip colour to them in fuchsia pills
until dawn wakes up the sponsor's big screen.
     When even a doorway must be muscular, a bank
slash hotel bulbous and vulgar as the railroad
man's image in three quarters mirror,
the blank side rufous and absorbent of the street,
               it's up to the likes of you
               to coin a strategy
               to stay awake and moral.
     Blinding light gives way
to nights deep as the one continuous sea hemming
your bit by brief houses, air counterpane
perpendicular to want reveals itself to be a sink
of unpaved water. Take cone from shelf, place
over head, and bang against the boards as you sleep, two by
four. You can still feel the warmth of a body in the water
though it is passing you quickly, whisked into foam.
Your dream of forcing the ground back
as that wild drop is condensed into inches, is bred
in the tanned basket of your groin, you knew that
body stripped becomes a bow, colour of a gram of milk,

wild as it retreats under cover the light
of its nerve writes silver
initials on air only you can see.   Your place is marked
by two bow-shaped metal handles,
here your lunch is, here you irradiated with news aspire
as a low whisks your frock, turned up
like the tulip bow to wind, your face turned
up to a cloudy gel that makes the blue
deep as a container port. Not like beams
chucked up, rusted, torn down, chucked
into parallel lines in yards, dispersing
into a medley of scarlet spots, but like the air
under which the rocks grind. You grind your face up. You spark.

THESE THINGS HAPPEN IN OUR HOMES

Toyle to prevent imaginary wants
who calls on me with her human voice
and when she did ring it was a cashback
offer on the female intrusive cancers.
Who lack a birdbath are covered by the sky,
                    that self same
              bevelled strap to   muse yourself on
The great dictator an interesting rhetorical figure,
weeds tickling between the ribs rock
the whole hat-stand with chortles, bugs
run out of   sky as historically conceived

delivers a series of bad eggs we were born out of
on which is calibrated every instrument.
The boys are testing with four near-perfect
spheres the potential for relative warps
In a clean way, the dragging of space into motion
Microdancers latest crazy child
a second educated detail
marked off like the face of a clock.

Well he *was* beaten to death but he was not a man.
More like a jack fruit razor, split
and stuffed in a styrofoam box   up-country
games for hunters on ice-skates took   Boredom
drives me, forceps, and desire
seen here in my knickers   The till lady says
'my loved one' to Peter with a fistful
beside her   a third of us hostile, arbitrary and inventive
eating through the building

The cropped girl with the camel-bone mirror
does not have on her face
that she will soon discover herself to be a mother.
Her hike on an ass a hail of
curses   of hock-crows
It was harder than we expected.
It was more abhorrent than we expected, more ... gushy.
Don't even *like* gays, what they do in their own homes.
Calling for his fringe, opposition getting harder,
lacing up the eyeholes of the dead with TV

tubes. If these things can be comprehended,
you're fucking orbit, air apparent, your fire engine lip
sticks   cover the trap   sealed with organic resin
of as-yet-unknown origin. Want to hurtle across the sky?
The dark gets to, and cold rushes up your bevelled edge.
If not, and you *lie*, then heaven help you
down from the optional gothic panorama. You curl up like
pellets in your loading bays. The whole will open up to you
as the trap clicks through each of its twelve stations.

Jeremy Reed

SUNGLASSES

The cool look, wide-screen Jackie O
blackouts in a circular frame,
eyewear like a tinted limo,

the car sealed like a mausoleum
flash outside Van Cleef & Arpels
for a laminated icon.

Jimmy Dean used shades as purdah,
thunder-black moodies airbrushing
a masochistic gay chutzpah.

Raybans were a Warhol fetish,
industrial, alien wraparounds
glossy as raindropped nail polish.

They're image-props to attitude,
enigma, iris-free disdain,
staging a Rothko solitude

like Kirk's originals, amber
octagonals graduating to brown
lenses, like leaf-turn September.

Mystique enhancers, Monroe-wear
to hide the bruises, or pushed up
as celeb pointers in the hair,

they're confirmation of a shift
away from centre, someone moved
into the corners, foggy drift.

With some it's drugs, desperado
cover for altered states, the light
burning in, punishing as snow.

With others it's summer romance.
The sea at Cap Ferrat tinted
a blue on blue. The sky in trance.

Matthew Francis

COFFEE AND GAULOISES

Last night in Mill Road the coffee shop
was closed. Only the smell was open,
filling the air. Language students sang

basking in the warmth of the coffee
that was a kind of weather now, freed
from any need to be drinkable,

or a foreign country whose borders
were unrolling further after dark
than they had ever reached in daylight.

*

This morning, coffee and Gauloise smoke
are probing the sector of my brain
I'd set aside for my hangover.

They are not to be separated
from each other, or from the vapours
last night's red wine has infumed me with.

They are the weather of a language
I don't speak. I can't look at its sun
or where it's shining from, that French blue.

Peter Robinson

THE EMPIRE OF LIGHT

for Giulia

When out of the subway we climbed, dusk's darkened
sky came to meet us
there in the form
of a mid-blue hue from the sun's afterlight
screened with warmly off-white clouds
that didn't seem to move at all
beyond a balconied grey house-end,
the darkly pointing leaves
and lamp lit above a linteled door
over that embassy wall . . .

You noticed!
and said so in the street by a bankrupt hotel's
annex where I stayed
those many years before
when a slight glimpse of the perimeter's fence
with flag limp on its pole
was sign enough to start up resentments or fears.
But here, as you're beside me
pointing at this blue,
I see now an embassy gloaming spells out
that even the impossible can happen too

– which is how it was with us, to say the least.

Alex Smith

ROME

There are moments in life
when even Schubert has nothing
to say to us.   – Henry James

I could never have dreamt so many years,
their burden. Even my skin . . . you know,
has turned ash-pale. We are passing out
of the frame. Baroque, rococo,
we worry so much about *style*. And yet
time is a string, a thread leading through ruins
that look as though they have never
been anything other than ruins.

Stop playing with your table napkin and listen.

We start to count the countries of Europe
but run out of time. Inconsequential.
Taxis swirl and stop, drop off, pick up.
We dine by the Forum tonight. It's all, somehow . . .
more elegant, more *romantic* in the rain.
(A screech as we scrape our metal chairs
on the pavement.) Waiters. Menus
opened with extravagant gestures.
They despise us. No, don't say anything. Shut
up. And don't stare at them. Remember,
there are no corners in eternity.

The plaster is crumbling in the hallway,
along the stairs. It's all so dimly lit.
You said she lived here. Well,
it's squalid, I'll tell you that.

For such the steady Romans shook the world:
coins, fountains.
Trash.

The Circus Maximus recedes into the sunset
like Turner's classical diminuendos.
The dogs are settling for the night,
nestling among the ruins, comfortable
with their own warmth and their own smell.

Do as I do and you'll be fine.
Look out at the station though – amputees,
women trading babies . . . they'll try anything.

Distribute the candles. Genuflect.
How can one know God in this darkness?

Tourist coaches line the avenue
with Dutch and Germans trailing through
the electric evening, exhausted.
You can't move for luggage. And here comes
that party still wearing their funny hats.

What is to be said, staring into the sun?
That all our betrayals and lusts are antique?

Come, we must go now.
Just look at the painted figures,
nearly falling out of the ceiling.

Carol Rumens

EXILE: AN UPDATE

A journey always meant hope.
When they rammed the truck black, and you couldn't retreat
from so much breath, none of it wanting yours:
when you paid a Mercedes for the back of a lorry,
when you dropped yourself from the top of the fence and bounced it
at the Eurostar, and stuck there like a skingraft
or suture, knees hands fingers soles an agony of stitching
through steel, and earth's long wound flying beneath,
that journey still meant hope – if you could hang on, if
your mind could: hope, the lick of water,
hope, with the face of your child
at the end of the tunnel.

Graduates of transport, you mastered arrival:
the gun-butted tumble straight to hell, or the scenic
route; the lie on the gate, the shrug in the street,
a street where you built a pram of the things that would be your life
when there were walls again, and form, and shadow,
or a street where you looked for a coin:
someone had always dropped a coin, if you looked
hard for the little shine.
This time, it's different again.
The light seems right, you already know some of the language.
The village greets you at last. It's beautiful:
the little hates are bricked and plumbed, the seepage
drip-feeds the perfect green.
You learn to wait, though nobody else is waiting.
You stand still, walk around the block, or stretch
carefully out on the pavement,
still hoping. But it's not
yours, that coin. It's ours. We lost it years ago,
you stole it. Look how strangely

it shimmers as you stare a thousand years down
in the island's mud. One kindly finger shows you
your place, the illegality, the proper
attitude, and the first flight home:
Another five say, Oi, Saddam, here's what
hope hoped, what journey journeyed to.

WELSH STREAM

We heard no watery rustle, saw no movement
at first. And then we spotted it, the tic,
the one-nerve flicker, every thirty seconds,
and knew, with an absurd sense of reprieve,
that the dead muscle, brown as parcel-seal,
where clay sagged at the weight of fern and horsetail,
was in fact living water, weak but striving
with tiny shudders for a different place.

Gordon Kennedy

WATER DUST

water dust
the taste of broken lightbulbs
static play of charge
starvd vacuum licking outward

he emerges from the furnace heart
in million neon
voice like thorn a tongue
of noise to tear white chiffon

:

& they have entered the petrified forest
a fire made of glass shards crackling
burdock, monkshood, rapeseed
where the branches mesh like a wing

& the slivers in the glassblowers' waste-pit
whisper on thru airconditioning forever
the geology of infinitesimals diamond grinding diamond
spiralinward to the blinded core

to the core of the nub of the heart of it

:

in a primary school of one
the maimed child dips her one toast soldier
over & over, into a dry white eggcup
hearing faintly something

or the wind \ a window shatters on the \
something imperceptibly
extend itself forever out
across the perfect field

AND THEY HAVE ENTERED WITHIN

sense floods upward thru the space behind

we are average men sir
  wheelchairs bound in skin
    the whir of bonewhite noise

                                                   we do not
                                                 wish
                                               to know

         floods upward thru the

  half past seven
    it is time now to
      electrocute the child

                              for this is how we teach it
                                   to electrocute
                                  the second child

      the man in the street shakes out his wet umbrella

        (only do
            our job we not
        exceptional)

      and walks into the building

earth inhabit me
  : my hands' red witness
    i have spoke with strangers

    and they have entered within
  : a dark like fingers
earth inherit me

      but in the street a man

    the magus now unlocks his ribcage
      with the ribkey
    to reveal a cracked white egg

      shakes out his black umbrella

    in the brokenwindowed sky
      a sun appears
     inside its moon

from which not one clear droplet falls imperfect

Paul Henry

THREE TREES

for J, J & I

I planted three trees, for privacy
and for feeling near to the soil.
Three ferns, two a fairer shade
of green, the middle one a clone
of my father's dark spire.
(One Spring, he swapped his violin
for a spade).

              I planted three trees.
Leisurely climbers, I loved them,
suddenly taller when I turned
to look at them again.
Perhaps I planted them too close.
The wind blows in from the sea
and they seem to conspire
against me.

              I planted three trees.
It snows. Sand hurries
through the kitchen's hourglass.
I am nearer the soil
than ever I intended to be.
Above me

              three, fern-haired men
point to the cold stars,
all is silence, but for a spade
played out of key.

Kieron Winn

THIRTIES

Galled at our loss of
Brightness, we awake in pairs
On these settled streets.

WORDSWORTH AND COLERIDGE

Insufficient, the broad
Oaten flakes,
The convictions plain
As Skiddaw –

How Coleridge would have loved
Neon, glutamates
And so many channels:
Intricate, hare-like, in the end a nuisance.

ROCK MUSIC IN A SHOP

The capitalist tattoo
And I want something:
A roaring crowd
And far from the shades
Some decent shades.

Blue sky, hard-domed;
The mass and curvature
Of a daylight moon.
Will, fuel, and time:
I am not dreaming.

Vona Groarke

IN PASSING

Maybe nothing now will pass on the lawn
but another hour, parading its gold chain,
clinking its shadows. Yesterday, it was a boy
in a baseball cap picking something yellow
from the grass. Tomorrow, perhaps a man
and woman, small-talk playing into their hands,
ignoring this window, my one taken liberty.
The same tense does for both, literally,
if not for what comes between them:
a darkness planted by me on a whim,
mindful of ink passing through my pen
to spill what's written on what will remain.

Carrie Etter

ELECTION

When wind grazed the fields and the sun gave kaleidoscopes meaning, we rallied behind our candidates. There was dew on the hydrangea, and scientists recorded the emissions of stars. Hoping the contender's heart most resembled our own, each of us loitered at the voting booth, each of us used a foot to draw shapes in the sand. Within hours the near-apocalypse sundered elements and earth, and the election ended in pure democracy: a trio of voices with scripts for a sextet.

Penelope Shuttle

THE WORLD

When you're so tired
you can't bear the world –

that's when you really begin to live,
when you're closest to the world

How difficult it is to love it,
unlike the moon at first light

carrying her weight so readily
But the world

longs for all it will never have again,
that's the world's heavyweight nature,

all its mountains have fear,
all its chasms have sadness

In rainy weary prime of life
the world endures its broad lawful wings of light,

not beautiful, not happy,
so tired you can't bear it, how the world is

IN THE KITCHEN

A jug of water
has its own lustrous turmoil

The ironing board thanks god
for its two good strong legs and sturdy back

The new fridge hums like a maniac
with helpfulness

I am trying to love the world
back to normal

The chair recites its stand–alone prayer
again and again

The table leaves no stone unturned
The clock votes for the separate burial of hearts.

I am trying to love the world
and all its 8000 identifiable languages

With the forgetfulness of a potter
I'm trying to get the seas back on the maps
where they belong,

secured to their rivers

The kettle alone knows the good he does,
here in the kitchen, loving the world,
steadfastly loving – see how easy it is, he whistles.

POSTCARDS

Death quietly washing his or her hands,
counting the stones of China,
the shoes of the world to come

Many thanks for your grief,
says Death,
for your cloud and your story,
says Death,

scrawling postcards
of the sunset
to all his friends

and wish oh wish you were here

Peter Redgrove

THE COUNT OF SOME ACCOUNT

A mass of beard and talon filled the coffin.
One tear was all she allowed herself.
A hush beamed from the cloudless portion of the sky;
She watched the little travelling silence sorrowfully,
Fatal to him.

They were on the high ground of the island where
A little grassy alp parts two peaks; on this coll
The mourners worried their fiddles or with tears on their cheeks
Wept into their hats. Yet that night the unbearded
Count walked, patrolling his battlemented chateau –

It was this habitation was his solid shadow,
And having rebuilt it in his image he could no longer be
Caught in a mirror, his reflection now
Towered on this hill, nor
Caught in a coffin, like the mortal folk,
Nor in the dust, not on the sunniest day; others
Could get lost in his corridors and wander there
Until he chose to let them out or bite them.

The kinswoman thought the funeral was all right
When the parson stopped talking and gave her leave to think
Where the Count might be found; she turned away
And entered the gates, seeking not his shade
But his actual body among the actual stones raised
Into the ancestral home created for her
High up, on the island; he, the soft Count
Beardless, without fangs, talonless, and yet
The Ancestor, the only one, who built
From the beginning for her alone.

TOPFACE, NETHERFACE, FROGFACE

The snow lay on the trees
Like the milk of them crystallised,
It lay in labyrinths;
A flash of lightning
Lit up the drawn blind.

She kept the port decanter on the piano:
Wood, metal, felt, leather, glass, wine machine;
The look of them controlled the room,
The tipple got into the music
Directly, with alacrity.
A green frog squatted on her throat.
She fingered the white mistletoe berries
Sticky as libido.

The green frog at her throat
Was cut from a single emerald,
The totem animal of creation-from-the-morass:
She had a smooth top face, and a frog face,
And a nether face, bearded, veiled and questionable.
She is embroidering a zodiac belt,
She would turn it daily
Around something inside her like the sun
(A wall within the walls on which is written
The fate of the world, and its laws)

And the dowry frog speaks from the blouse
And netherface concurs
Saying among all else
That she is not pregnant yet,
Only ready to talk about it avers
Topkiss under the mistletoe.

PARADISE OF STORMS

Pepper and salt stubble, little
                    white crystals mixing with
                                        tiny black ones, this crystalline
Scum expounds into its beard,
                    the waves of beard
                                        flowing out of the skin
Ceaselessly, day and night, registering
                    by a small agitation of growth
                                        as the trees do
The presence of women
                    and the growth-properties
                                        of the weather.
Thus the beards, and the trees:
                    this one knows that a woman
                                        waited under it an hour today
During the rain; if we took
                    a slice of its trunk
                                        and looked carefully
At the fattening of the cambium
                    which registers the shower we would see
                                        a small figure with a furled
Umbrella. In a man
                    that would be a barbarity,
                                        can I read that lady
In the unfurling of my beard?
                    But the tree-rings should be read
                                        without broaching the bark
For the perfume of a tree
                    compiles its experience
                                        as it matures . . .

The great detective pauses
                    under the tree full of eyes
                              in the garden of the murder-house
And the name of the butcher
                    passes into his mind
                              like a whispering witness,
He lays his hand on the culprit's shoulder
                    whose beard reeks bloody murder
                              and an at-last-I-am-caught-and-
Can-rest blend of scents. Now
                    the paradise of storms passes on,
                              showering in every skin.

MOTH-ER

A sudden rose-garden in the bedroom.
                    I pad my way
                              through this labyrinth
To where she is.
                    As we kiss and touch our quick
                              windows open to the sky,
Which signal to her, finish.
                    Every dusk she eats a moth, it is
                              a winged key to the invisible,
It trembles on her tongue,
                    accepting her
                              as though she were the night
And the stars would bloom in her mouth
                    when this tiny
                              giving-of-all was enacted,
By moth-kiss, by moth-death. This
                    was her sin,
                              she had got her sins down
To this small murder
                    and the eating up of this
                              little star-map . . .
Her figure reclining in violin-shape,
                    a little bonfire on the tongue,
                              her dozing body pulses
As though the skin were moths,
                    their tones. She
                              sees through her skin
With a moth's eyes and with
                    its radio tuned to moth-death,
                              the final broadcast . . .

Completely insupportable,

                the quicksilver-flutter,

                    the burst of rank juice

Like a turpentine, like tasting

                a painter's brush in starlight . . .

Which paints stars

                arranged in their cupolas

                    like whispering galleries

Crowded with white-faced watchers.

                She licks this brush for luck:

                the star

Painted across the moth's back

                reappeared in heaven.

                Now her skin is soft

As as many moths as she's consumed, fitted together

                in galactic designs of touch;

                    this is the secret she gives to me,

The winged jewels built into a temple,

                with her last breath

                    as conscious mind and the

                        unconsciousness

Rush together, and the stench or perfume

                in her last breath seeks above

                    its constellation of the Mother,

Moth.

Essay

The *Poetry Review* Essay

MATT FFYTCHE

Fashion

It's a difficult task selling fashion to poets, especially British ones. The difficulty is not, of course, that poetry is unwilling to connect with beautiful things – but that these are meant to be enduring, not just the latest fad. A thing of beauty, we are reliably informed, is not a passing fancy but "a joy forever". Certainly the objects of poetic veneration are not meant to be so obviously and merely for sale. In America, arguably, it's a different story. John Wieners at one point considered the general editorship of *Vogue* magazine, while Charles Bernstein, in *The Sophist*, recollects how his father "pushed a / line of ladies dresses". Hard to think of similar instances in the UK, where a line of thought running from Keats through Arnold to T. S. Eliot has insisted, in its thinking about beauty, on a sense of timelessness completely at odds with the rapid modulations of fashion. *Four Quartets* evokes a condition of complete simplicity that would be "here, now, always", at the same time as "costing not less than everything". Prufrock, meanwhile, was uncertain whether to wear his trousers rolled.

All this contrasts greatly with France, where poetry and fashion have been in each other's pockets ever since Baudelaire sacralised the urbane glamour of the city, along with speed, boredom and the spectacle of the everyday. Fashion, he wrote, is a symptom of "the taste for the ideal that floats on the surface in the human brain". It's a pact that was modeled on the boulevards of the Second Empire, and later sported more jauntily by Apollinaire and Blaise Cendrars. Even so, Mallarmé is the only poet I can think of who went so far as to edit his own fashion journal. Called *La Dernière Mode* (the latest fashion), it launched in the autumn of 1874 in an edition of 3000 and ran for eight fortnightly issues until the proprietor, Charles Wendelen, took the project out of his hands shortly before Christmas. A whimsical little enterprise, you'd think, undertaken by someone who was routinely short of cash. But there's more to the story than that, for not only was Mallarmé the editor, he was also its principle columnist, Madame de Ponty, as well as Ix, its cultural reviewer, and its reporter Miss Satin. In fact, just about everything in the magazine – bar, ironically enough, the literary pieces – was written under a variety of pseudonyms by Mallarmé himself. The events listings of operettas and *tableaux vivants* are his, as are the menus for hunt luncheons and checklists of fashionable bathing resorts, and the recommendations to see the "extraordinary skaters Goodrich and Curtis". Above all, there are Mallarmé's original fashion designs – miniature poetic artifacts themselves: "Skirt in navy-blue silk. Tunic in cashmere of the same shade, with puffed folds and lining of turquoise silk. Little diagonal pieces of navy-blue silk on the folds and round them. The bodice has two points and is in cashmere with silk trimming in two tones. All this ornamented with black pearled lace." One can hardly imagine Yeats, for all his interest in Byzantine filigree, coming up with tips for interior decoration such as that given by Marliani (Mallarmé again) on how to adapt gas to Dutch-style Jewish lamps to create a "clear and polished ring of six radiant bronze burners". Each is now a horizontal jet of light "able to supply continuous gas in the cavity which used to hold the evening's oil".

How should we take this? Was the whole thing a very intricate private joke? Was it an attempt to make high art more streetwise? Was it even, as some have suggested, an orphic masterwork written in cryptic allegorical code? Not surprisingly, ever since its republication amongst Mallarmé's collected works, *La Dernière Mode* has been somewhat sidelined, either as too trivial, or too obscure, to warrant much attention. But this first complete translation of Mallarmé's contributions[1] (strangely, still ahead of any large-scale translation of his critical writings on poetics) provides ample opportunity to review the whole fashion question and its curious presence at the sidelines of Mallarmé's work. To turn the tables around somewhat (the tables being black lacquer, inlaid with chameleons in mother of pearl, available on offer from Bon Marché), I could point out that these criticisms of triviality and obscurity levelled at *La Dernière Mode* are precisely the same that had been levelled at Mallarmé's poetry itself, ever since he had begun to publish in the *Parnasse contemporain* of 1865. For the brothers Goncourt, Mallarmé was either insane, or a charlatan. Henri Ghéon had him down for a hoaxer, while Max Nordau, in *French Contemporaries*, described him as a "lamentable eunuch with a weak mind". So much for the opposition. But even his own associate, Catulle Mendès, recalled Mallarmé reading out a text "so intractably obscure that he could scarcely keep from laughing". More recent academic admirers, such as Malcolm Bowie, have likewise had to qualify the attractions of the poetry. It's not just that he does not say what he means, writes Bowie, but that "difficulty can sometimes appear as a gratuitous cult of indirectness, a box of tricks, a fad". A merely fashionable obscurity, perhaps? Which leaves Mallarmé with the double taint of the crypt and the coffee table.

---

1. *Mallarmé on Fashion: A Translation of the Fashion Magazine La Dernière Mode*, with Commentary, ed. and tr. P.N.Furbank and A.M. Cain, Berg, £15.99, ISBN 1859737234.

But there is a stronger case to be made for the link between poetry and fashion. In fact, I'd go so far as to say that fashion and poetry, for Mallarmé, form part of a single brocade. Take the subjects of many of Mallarmé's most famous sonnets: what are they? A piece of lace ("Une dentelle s'abolit"); interior furnishings ("Ses purs ongles"); a fan ("Autre Éventail"). "Nothing can ever rival a fan, with a setting as rich as you please or quite simple, but affirming, above all, ideality", quips *La Dernière Mode*'s domestic goddess Madame de Ponty. Or think of a swan's feathers trapped in ice, from one of Mallarmé's most famous productions, "Le vierge, le vivace et le bel aujourd'hui". Don't we find Madame again insistently plugging tulle, "especially white" with a ragged edge, for the Christmas season, giving "a charming illusion of feathers", and likewise dresses "trimmed in frost-flowers – blonde lace encrusted with white jet", or hats "all white, with plume and white wing"? Correspondingly, many of the descriptions in *La Dernière Mode* conjure up, even for Mallarmé himself, nothing so much as ... a poem by Mallarmé. Take this description of Madame Ratazzi, famous Parisian hostess, whose hair "was pulled up in a diadem, with four strings of enormous diamonds intertwined in its shade and buried in its dark splendour" – a miraculous vision which suggests to the columnist "certain impressions, deep or fleeting, of the poet". I wonder which poet she had in mind. More of diamonds in the dark anon.

What are we to make of this thrusting together of two worlds – high art and fashion, poetry and commodification – that modern poets, especially in Britain, have struggled to keep apart? Is it "To teach the beauty in everyday things", as the magazine early on suggests? Or are none of these voices to be trusted? Is it all arch – a clever if somewhat elaborate way of *épater les bourgeois?* Another paean to whiteness, this time from Miss Satin, seems to shout the latter. Whiteness plays a complex role in Mallarmé's work, at one and the same time a symbol for the purity of ideas as well as the void beneath human experience, and also the blank sheet before which the poet despairs over these alternatives. But, for Miss Satin, whiteness

appears in the form of snow and cream, and "these two quite contrary whitenesses, for me, combine their virtues without their danger, in the product delightfully named Crème-Neige". Poetry as … skin cream? At least we know where we stand. Scarves with pink buttons embroidered in tartan, or hair bows in two shades – "nasturtium and sulphur-yellow" or "steely-blue and iron-grey" – are Mallarmé's version of pied beauty.

To gain a deeper understanding of Mallarmé's motives here, we have to place his world of "a thousand charming whimsies", of life's "tremendous trifles", amongst the consumer spectacles of the Third Republic. This is partly the world which Walter Benjamin sought to exhume in his Parisian Arcades Project, which charts, amongst many other things, the birth of the department store, the construction of Haussmann's boulevards and the metropolitan modifications of lyric poetry. Or rather, it is its cosmetically enhanced heir. As Benjamin's work is centred around Baudelaire and the 1850s, Mallarmé's Paris is that world raised to a higher power: taken over by consumer extravaganzas, speeded up, running on empty. Mallarmé himself has a fleeting presence in Benjamin's notes, caught obliquely in sections dealing with mirrors, idleness, and fashion. It is a world in which the "world" itself has already been subsumed as a branch of consumerism. For Mallarmé, there is nothing so strange but Paris will accept it, "nothing exquisite that it cannot offer for sale." It is fashion which now projects the map of the modern cosmos.

What are the features of this world? What are the conditions set down for any poetic rendition of human existence? Firstly, it is a world in which all traces of a "nature" that is not primped and tagged for human consumption have been vaporised. It is "not natural to be what is called 'natural' any longer", conceded Arthur Symons in his brief essay on Mallarmé. Another of Mallarmé's handy tips for "changing rooms" is to embed a fish-tank in a panelled wall and fill it with "polypuses, starfish, Japanese telescope-fish …" (the list is a poem in itself). That way one acquires an aquarium that is magical, moving, and extraordinary, but with the added bonus of "a shelf with drawers below". If Parisians still feel the need to make that trip to Normandy, seeking rest for the eyes "in the oblivion of a vast and naked horizon", they should not deceive themselves about the pleasure that really awaits them, which is that of feasting their eyes on "a new fashion: the paradox of the toilettes, simple yet sophisticated, embroidered by the ocean with its waves".

Another running joke in the magazine is Mallarmé's evocation of what fashion does to time. Ix, the reviewer, pauses to consider the oddity of writing a "Paris Chronicle" when the magazine has no past – "For we arrive on the scene unknown, with only a future." But this only sets up the punchline for Madame de Ponty who elsewhere suggests that, "our eyes dazzled by irisations, opalisations or scintillations, how are we to focus so vague a scene as the Future?" And as for the present – "to have the permanence of a tulle illusion … that is one's dream for every sentence one writes … about the news of the day". Or as Mallarmé reworks this in "Crisis in Poetry": "a present does not exist… Ill-informed anyone who would announce himself his own contemporary".

Fashion inaugurates a curious suspension of reality. As much as Mallarmé's world is saturated with news and spectacle and opinion and distinction – as is our own – it is, in effect, incapable of displaying its own substance or history. What emerges instead is a constantly recycled swirl of images which circulate as so much ornamental detritus: fashion as the charnel house of decayed cultural motifs. As Madame de Ponty notes in the first issue, her readers are "living in an epoch when all creative force has disappeared…

we are thrown back upon exhumations." For Benjamin, the extremes of fashion were exemplified by frivolity and death. Mallarmé goes one step further. For him, death itself now raises a serious fashion dilemma. On All Souls Day he notes an embarrassment about funerary matters and wonders if, due to the increasing dominance of ashes, "the Tomb may not come to be considered an outmoded curiosity". Tombs, of course, are an important anchorage point for recollection. Mallarmé wrote his own "tombs" for Poe, Verlaine, and Baudelaire. If tombs go out of fashion, does that make memory itself unfashionable?

It is tempting to locate some of these obliterations of past and future in relation to the political traumas of the early 1870s. Mallarmé finally made the move to Paris from the provinces in October 1871 – just a year after the catastrophic rout of the French army at the battle of Sedan with the subsequent siege of Paris, and only a few months after the bloody reduction of the Paris Commune which saw over 20,000 Parisians killed in one May week. Even though, shortly after this, Mallarmé himself was off to London on a journalistic mission to cover the Great Exhibition, these events cannot fail to haunt the spectacles of *La Dernière Mode*. Sure enough, we find the trace of these suppressed horrors glaring through the phantasmagoria of the present. In a passage which is both supremely arch, and poignant for the reality it knowingly displaces, Mallarmé comments of the predicted "invasion" of tourists in August: "I would prefer to see them, those strange couples with their patriarchal beards or uncurled hair, studying through their binoculars, the disappearance of the great city, see it eclipsed, dead, abolished, a heap of cinders and weeds, rather than making themselves at home in it." Likewise, he notes how "those facades, with their statuettes still, after three years, blackened by fire" are visited now "by young persons in white-veiled Tyrolean hats".

What is at issue here is a double devastation, however. Certainly there's the illicit memory of the trauma of war and revolution which the new "republic" has tried to plunge into oblivion. But then there's the oblivion which permeates the attempt at recovery itself, the cocquetry of a metropolis "audaciously new, rich and splendid", as the magazine boasts. The tenor of the new epoch emerges in nothing so much as the gala opening of the New Opera House in January 1875. In "Crisis in Poetry", Mallarmé proclaimed that a people "bears witness to its transfiguration in truth". But this truth, perhaps under the vogueish influence of Wagner, will be "the playing out of festivals". Such festivals and spectacles flood the pages of the fashion magazine, including the penchant for sumptuous historical dramas – *The Queen of Sheba*, *Mary Queen of Scots* – as well as the popular stage version of Jules Verne's "Journey Around the World". At the same time, Mallarmé is forced to note "what a catastrophe is a whole evening of our existence lost in that cave of cardboard and painted canvas" if nothing is worth the attention, "the living marionettes declaim their loud nonsense before us . . . against a background of exasperated boredom." Literary action, "does not transgress this theatre".

So where does this leave the poet, who recognises, as he saunters through the "shoe-shops of the book", the assimilation of the writer to the twists and turns of the marketplace? Is poetry to become merely another fashion accessory to be left conspicuously on the sofa, or "banished to a lacquered cupboard, joining jewel boxes"? The 1876 deluxe edition of *L'après-midi d'un faun*, with its cover in white felt and the plates tied with silk tassels in pink and black, springs to mind.

Well, for a start, it leaves him or her with an irremediable sense of emptiness. This is one of the most famous facts about Mallarmé, his seeming loss of himself, and his conviction of the world's absurdity over a few dark months in 1866, which left him "perfectly dead", or perhaps reborn in nothingness. The crisis is often presented as a poetic rite of passage, marking his departure from the common world and his entrée as enigmatic hierophant of the symbolist clique. Famous, too, is his sense, in the midst of this crisis, of words reduced to bare aural vibrations – human language exposed in its essential rhythms. At points he reported having "forgotten the meaning of the most familiar words". By which I take it that the English-language teacher was not losing his grip on the French lexicon as such, but that the meanings of words had come to seem so purged of any stable referential context, so void of substance, that they sometimes presented themselves to his mind as mere sounds. "To utter the word so as to reimmerse it in its own futility" is one of the directions in his critical notes to *Igitur*.

Sartre's polemical and somewhat psycho-biographical work on Mallarmé – subtitled "The Poet of Nothingness" – is persuasive on the explosive internal mix of impotence and absolute defiance which leads Mallarmé to place the world in

brackets; which leads him to the point "where he sometimes believes that he has in fact killed himself". Sartre is good, too, on the epochal role this new stance will come to play in modern literature. "Mallarmé," he points out, "was the first to raise the still-timely question: 'Does anything like literature actually exist?'" From that moment, he goes on, "there has been no writer, however modest, who has not put the Word itself into question." What he misses here, though, is the portrait of Mallarmé's Paris, and the world of commerce rushing impetuously through it, that makes it such a fashionably changing – and ultimately insubstantial – place. Valéry, too, noted this changeableness, the "switching – at high frequency – of the tastes of a given public, which is called Fashion", and was a sign "that commercial interests were creeping in". Mallarmé's absolutely precarious and shimmering universe, in which "Every Thought Gives Forth A Throw of the Dice" (that translation courtesy of a youthful Frank O'Hara, before he had discovered Second Avenue) bears a close relation to the equally paradoxical and tortuous vision of eternity, chance, substance, and lies that would take hold within the later Nietzsche. And one supposes the same condition is at stake: the attempt to coin the new spiritual discourse of humanity at the very point where it becomes clear that no one can any longer marshal the terms of significance in the face of fashion's restless need for exchange. In some ways, Max Nordau was as near the truth as Sartre when he panned Mallarmé as "the poet who produces nothing" and compared his work to the period of swindles such as the South Sea Bubble on the London Stock Exchange.

The double bind is that, in the new era ushered in by modernity, the poet was to claim a public function as the prophet of a purely humane religion; a religion which sought to emblazon rather than transcend the everyday. But the everyday that unfolded – after 1848, and more fluently after 1871 – is one in which the erstwhile liberal vision of collectivity was increasingly sidelined and finally expunged by the motors of liberal commerce. This is what lead Benjamin to suggest that, with Mallarmé and the theory of *poesie pur*, "the cause of his own class has become so far removed from the poet that the problem of a literature without an object becomes the centre of the discussion". Hence the poetry's tendency to hinge on terms such as *blanc, absence, silence, vide*. Mallarmé himself, in interview, confirmed that "In an unstable society, lacking in unity, no stable and definitive art can be created". What is left then, as his brief essay on "Displays" puts it, is "an adroit oscillation" between forms of public and private emptiness – "promiscuity and the void"; or, as he suggested even more terrifyingly in "Mystery in Literature": "the raising up in rubble, standing there, of blindness without end". It's *The Waste Land*, but without any clutching of roots.

If one reads poetry and fashion out of and into each other, their points of coincidence become ever sharper. As a culture is slowly purged of dependable meanings, the poet's former canopy of stars, archetypes, and eternal symbols drifts towards a new set of terms: the poet's words become "jewels", obdurate fragments, bereft of any supportive context or necessary constellation, but unable to stop reflecting imagination's desire for meaning. Hence the celebrated description of how the poet now "yields his initiative to words, which are mobilized by the shock of their difference; they light up with reciprocal reflections like a virtual stream of fireworks over jewels". Or this from *Igitur*: "a null jewel of reverie, rich and useless survival, except that upon the marine and stellar complexity of a worked gold the infinite chance of conjunctions was to be read".

Words, prised from contexts of social commitment, have taken on an abstract life of their own. "Its meaning if it has one", wrote Mallarmé of his poem "Ses purs ongles", "is conveyed through a hidden mirage suggested by the words themselves". One sees here the beginnings of that immense artistic

turn, partly inaugurated by Mallarmé, towards abstraction – not only in poetry, but also in art and music and performance in the twentieth century. But (and this is surely the key point), one also sees how this movement, far from representing an ivory tower mentality – the rejection of the "outside" for the refined enclosure of a private religion – is actually very closely interconnected with the rhythms and rationale of that world. For it is precisely at this point of abstraction that poetry reflects the operation of fashion, which is likewise uprooting and destabilizing reality, turning everything into spectacle. As words become jewels, like the strings of diamonds drawn up into the hair of Madame Ratazzi, we are returned to our starting point, because these jewels conjure up nothing so much as the glittering vortex of the *belle époque*. Indeed, Madame de Ponty's first editorial is on jewellery. But the point, which I hope will flash out from this essay, is that poetry's conjunction with the world of fashion here is not about abandoning significance for show, but the opposite. As with Mallarmé's close involvement with Manet's work, it is about cleaving to the significance of the world at hand, rather than drawing a protective veil over it. Perhaps one might add that only a poetry which can look the shattering of the everyday in the eye, is also able to resist it.

All illustrations on the preceding pages are reproduced from *Mallarmé on Fashion, A Translation of the Fashion Magazine La Derniere Mode, with Commentary*, ed. and tr. P. N. Furbank and A. M. Cain, Berg, 2004, by permission of the publisher.

Poetry Review / **Whitechapel Gallery readings**

John Wilkinson and Helen Macdonald

11 November, 2004

7pm, Free admission

Whitechapel Art Gallery
80-82 Whitechapel High Street
London E1 7QX

Reviews

Don't look back

Deryn Rees-Jones, *Quiver*,
Seren, £9.99, ISBN 1854113542

Deryn Rees-Jones's book-length detective-story poem plays with concepts of authorship and influence. It is reminiscent of a Paul Auster novel in that layers of storylines echo and double-back on each other, both inviting and evading interpretation. As is the case in so many of Auster's stories, the narrator is a writer. Here, the writer (Fay) discovers the dead body of her husband's ex-lover, Mara, and tries to solve the mystery of her murder. She is also battling with writer's block, and her attempt to discover who Mara was becomes a search for a kind of muse. One of the poems which gets written along the way is central to the book as a whole, and takes its title, "Quiver".

"Quiver" tells the story of the hunter-goddess Artemis, also known as Diana, and the boy-hunter, Actaeon. The main source for the story is Ovid's *Metamorphoses* but other versions are mentioned, such as Titian's "Diana and Actaeon". The writer of "Quiver" playfully draws attention to the fact that this is a retelling of a well-known myth by using five false beginnings: "let's start with the stag"; "let's start with the head at the feet of the huntsman"; "let's start with … a young man", and so on. She then echoes Ovid by naming each of Actaeon's hounds, which in this version become iconic women, almost a female canon:

> Millicent, Sylvia,
> Christabel, Emily, Angel Virginia, No-nonsense Simone,
> Glorious Gloria, Unblushing Germaine;
> Fierce Luce, Brave Julia, La belle Hélène.

Artemis would appear to head the list: she famously turned Actaeon into a stag when he discovered her bathing naked in a forest stream, and caused him to be torn apart by his own hounds. In Ovid's version, as the goddess of chastity, her motivation is to prevent Actaeon from telling anyone what he saw, which of course doesn't work: each time the story is retold, her nudity is described all over again. Lethal though she is, Artemis cannot subvert "the male gaze". But in this retelling, a new perspective is introduced, personified by a character called Faith. Faith – "airing the flex and taughtness of her limbs"– does not mind being seen. Her name is deliberately close to Fay, that of our narrator/detective. She wants to return the stare:

what she wanted
was to look at the man without fear or shame
with an image of herself with which to begin.

The impulse to re-examine stories and storylines recurs throughout the book. A pair of cartoon-strip policemen "practice their clichés till they know them by heart". In "Flashback" a remembered photograph of Mara turns into a false memory of her preparing a meal. A return to the scene of the crime finds the writer asking herself: "What do I want? / For words and worlds / to unwrite themselves?". And when she has to tell her husband about Mara's murder she faces the impossibility of conveying her news in these breathless lines: "how will it be when / I have to tell him / when this narrative arrests / and the past opens / and time wobbles / and what I have to tell / becomes at once too long, too short?" ("The Story of a Life").

The husband, Will, is a geneticist, and, with two pregnancies occurring in the story, links are made between the birth of an idea and a biological conception. A pregnancy unleashes creativity: "A life flutters and turns inside …. / words spill across an empty page". Myriad reproductive techniques are praised in "Beatitude", from spirogyra's conjugation to "the cool pipette". "Clone" is not quite a clone but a variation of Paul Muldoon's parison "As" (from *Moy Sand and Gravel*). It even contains a cheeky acknowledgement of its progenitor –

As….

… Moy becomes moi
so this becomes you –

and climaxes in biological conception –

As…

vagina becomes penis, flowering in the shadowy womb
so this becomes you.

Set-piece poems such as this are skilfully interspersed throughout the narrative, providing a break from the story without diminishing the reader's desire to know what happens next. This elastic structure allows for a refreshing variety of tone and pace, and the book opens with fluid, economical free verse that places the reader right in the position of the narrator:

a blackbird opens its feathery throat
pulling the sky and the skyline closer
so hedgerow and barbed wire and railing,

the crunch of my footsteps on glistening paths
rise up together, clash and unite,

when suddenly I stumble, hit the ground.

("The Cemetery")

At other, scene-setting moments, unusual images help to pin down a sense of place and atmosphere. The kneeling congregation at Mara's funeral is "a row of question marks interrogating darkness, / a shaft of sudden light". There are also pleasing refrains that help to reveal the arc of the story. Part III opens with the last line of the first poem: "Everything's still". And twice we're invited away from the pull of what-happens-next to observe the season: "Green shoots spike the frost / like secrets, promises that haunt us" ("A Change in the Weather").

Happily, this subtle storyteller complements rather than replaces the Deryn Rees-Jones of *The Memory Tray* and *Signs Around a Dead Body*. "Relics", the penultimate poem, is a characteristic love poem which meanders through the quietly beautiful images of stars and snow that suffuse these earlier collections. Perhaps it also reveals a way in which Fay, at least, can acknowledge both male and female influences in her writing:

And so the soft straightforward night
begins with snowfall, snowdrifts – or do we just imagine that –
as winter's ending colours us, imagines us as people
we have never been. And though a thousand different stories
quiver in a moment – a hand unclasped, a darting word unsaid –
I don't look back. Familiar in a dream
somewhere, my cheek pressed to your shoulder,
our lives grow up between us. Like the glistening bones
of martyrs, saints, you hold about your person,
I remind you, as we drive "This is our tale",
and words our only keepsakes of the Bluebird's journey home.

JANET PHILLIPS

Inside from the start

Ken Smith, *You Again: Last Poems and Other Words,*
Bloodaxe, £8.95, ISBN 1852246707

Ken Smith's poetry is crammed with information: people, places, dates. Consider this, from "Late night call", the first poem in *You Again*:

> Discontinued voice from a disconnected number
> in a distant rainy Seattle, you're sitting on a balcony,
> smoking in another no-smoking house, out there
> in the time zones. We're out of sync.

At once, the reader is drawn into something dramatic and urgent; required to stake a claim. By the time most contemporary poems reach us, the "intolerable wrestle with words and meanings" is over: the poem is a score-card. As might be expected from a seasoned traveller, Smith's poems are closer to a list of essentials.

Proceeding by intuition means you can cover ground more quickly. Smith placed a high value on coincidence, or more precisely, synchronicity. In one of the interviews transcribed in *You Again*, Smith says:

> what we see is only the surface, and the deeper meaning, the deeper substance of what is going on can sometimes be recognised through signs, multiple feelings, symbols, feelings you have about places, people, things, and that one has to trust these feelings as much as one trusts analytical thought. One of the ways is to recognise coincidence…

Smith draws heavily on these perceived equivalences between cultures, or over long time periods: "Nothing has changed … toothache felt like toothache, sexual craziness like sexual craziness". Sometimes the assumed equivalence between the prison wall and the Berlin wall, or between victims of communism and capitalism, can sound simplistic, but more often it leads to an inspired clarity. Volume by volume, Smith found common ground with an ever more diverse set of characters. *Wild Root* is beautifully orchestrated – Smith's most coherent volume – yet also has the most eclectic terms of reference: the American Deep South is set against post-Communist Eastern Europe and Serbian myth. Because Smith's vision as a poet grew more coherent the more he broadened his range, he found himself with more and more to say.

Synchronicity, equivalence. Take, for example, the accident of one's name. Kenneth John Smith is an absurdly common name, and a source of great amusement for the poet of Everyman ("Your Majesty / my name is Smith…"). In *Last Poems* we are told, "Bin Laden is Ken Smith" (the poem was occasioned by a fortuitous Internet find), and a poem in *Wormwood* is subtitled "for John and all the men in the world called John". Tongue-in-cheek perhaps, but when Smith plays it straight, the results can be hallucinatory. This is from "Part of the crowd that day", in which we hear the voice of anonymity itself:

> They were townsfolk, craftsmen, shopkeepers,
> The labouring poor who came in from the fields.
> They watched the witches burn, the heretics.
> They watched the ships leave for the Americas.
> They were on the bridge at Sarajevo the first time.
> They saw. They wondered. They shouted
> *burn her, hang him, slaughter the Albigensians.*

This common touch is the corollary of Smith's famous sympathy with outcasts and wanderers, a sympathy not based on shared experience so much as attitude, or something in the timbre of the voice itself, a dissipated syntax that marks out territory rather than paints a landscape. Like King Lear's Poor Tom, Smith's wanderers (Fox, the wanderer Yacob, Charlie Delta, Eddie and the rest) carry the conscience of the society that excludes them. Not that Smith ever sounds civic-minded. But it is not so much outsiders as insiders who fascinate Smith: prisoners, subjects of political despots, victims of the secret police or the capricious global economy. It emerges that those whom history overlooks are also the ones who internalise history's conflicts and divisions most deeply.

In a review of *Shed* (for *Stride* magazine) Martin Stannard complained

> I think it would be awfully easy to say something pleasantly
> politically correct about these poems and shrink from saying
> that these 300 pages demonstrate that Ken Smith does what he
> does very well but it's a bit samey after a while…

This needs to be addressed. So many characters make their way through Ken Smith's poetry, and clearly all of them contain a measure of Smith himself – as they must. Whether you have a problem with this depends on how you define a persona. A persona can be used as a disguise or as a theatrical mask. A disguise preserves the wearer's identity, a mask accentuates certain characteristics. There is a tradition in Bali (Smith doesn't refer to it, but I suspect he was aware of it), that an actor must find a correlation between his own face and that of the mask he wears: must laugh or cry with the mask. And not through an excess of zeal, but in order to ensure the overall body language is correct, to aid the performance. Likewise, there are fine movie actors who submerge themselves entirely in a role: method actors like De Niro. Then there are truly great actors who, at their best, risk revealing something of themselves. Smith was the Brando type: able to speak for so many, yet always unmistakably himself.

If all of this makes Smith sound rather too earnest, I should say that throughout *You Again*, the poet's peculiar brand of absurdist black humour is to the fore. In the prose poem "The 72 virgins question", some pertinent questions are asked, concerning the belief held by the September 11 hijackers that, as martyrs, they could look forward to the attentions of 72 virgins in paradise:

> How was the figure 72 arrived at? ... Are any of them boy virgins? What proportion, if any? ... Given the length of eternity, how long, and how, do they remain virgins? ... What if the martyr is a woman? Does she get the same privileges, and how does that go down with the lads back at the base?

This Brechtian humour can be traced to Smith's obsession with borders, whether geographical, historical or psychological. Increasingly, Smith opened up the borders of genre. When a poet has the confidence to allow humour into the mix, it lends great warmth to the work.

The poetry collected in *The Poet Reclining* and *Shed* is politically engaged, amused, sane and horrified. As well as opening new perspectives on this work, *You Again* contains Ken Smith's final poems, along with interviews, letters and some absorbing accounts of how he came to write key poems. Smith is refreshingly honest about his working methods, and talks of "slapping the poem around ... like a piece of pastry". There are tribute poems from Tom Pickard, Sean O'Brien, Michael Anania, Tony Connor and Judi Benson, many written in Smith's own manner, and a fine overview of his career by Roger Garfitt. The book also contains several photographs. There is a pronounced contrast between the warmth of the snapshots showing Smith relaxing with friends, and the publicity shots, in which Smith remains defiantly unknowable behind tinted spectacles, hat and moustache. Whether pose, publicity stunt or in-joke, these now appear part of Smith's great mask project.

PAUL BATCHELOR

Knives for crutches

Charles Simic, *Selected Poems 1963–2003*,
Faber, £12.99, ISBN 0571222722

Were someone prosaic enough to want poetic language like a pane of glass, they might be tempted to reach for some Charles Simic. Simic's plain style, his chaste diction, his lack of complex syntax or ear-catching effects, can read like a pruning back of artifice in order to reveal the image and the world. Simic was born in Belgrade in 1938 and emigrated to the United States in 1954, and he has translated numerous poets from the former Yugoslavia. With this in mind, Simic's own verse might seem the sort that has least to lose in translation. But peer at it longer, and the glass of his poetic language turns more opaque. Simic's verse attempts to represent the pre- and extra-linguistic: the world of the senses, dream and memory, and the world of objects, whilst acknowledging some of the difficulties involved in such an enterprise. The language is frequently self-referential, its splashes of colloquial colour a way of highlighting how idiom reveals itself and its habitual users as much as what may lie behind and beyond itself. Moreover, while the content of the poems may owe much to the likes of Lalic and Popa, their words are always in dialogue with an American tradition which includes Dickinson, Roethke and Stevens.

Charles Simic's method is reminiscent of the bric-a-brac surrealism of the artist Joseph Cornell, to whose work Simic dedicated his 1992 book *Dime-Store Alchemy*. Objects, collected and placed in one of Cornell's boxes, relate to one another and to the space around them. They are emblems of the psyche, but remain things found, not made, by the box's arranger. Simic's poems likewise frame a few striking images that can function as archetype, fetish or memento. The language of the poem may sometimes seem just a box to put these in; yet it will often alert one to the wordliness of a poem and the thingness of things. A glove, a shirt, a pencil or a fork may be defamiliarised. However, Simic is not so much concerned with making strange as with uncovering the truth of objects: the differing ways they may be apprehended and how they are in themselves. In this, and in other aspects of his work, Simic is a disciple of Heidegger. But, though occasionally words come with an implicit Heideggerian freight, in practice the poems often seem no more or less philosophical than are riddles and fresh metaphors. As Ted Hughes said of Vasko Popa:

the sophisticated philosopher is also a primitive, gnomic spell-maker. The desolate view of the universe opens through eyes of childlike simplicity and moody oddness.

Simic has learnt from surrealism, but his poems tend either to the strange archetypal imagery of folk literature, to a reawakening of the mundane, or to grotesque reminders of the mangled nature of reality. "A Landscape with Crutches" sounds like the title of a painting by Dali. Yet "the ants on their toy crutches / And the wind on its ghost crutch" are a prelude to:

> The bread on its artificial limbs,
> A headless doll in a wheelchair,
> And my mother, mind you, using
> Two knives for crutches as she squats to pee.

As crutches give way to artificial limbs and a wheel-chair, so crutches cease to be dreamy archetypes and are sharpened for re-use. For all that they invite a Freudian reading, such images point back out to reality, to Simic's memories of Yugoslavia in the Second World War and to the atrocities of the present, quite as much as they point inwards to the unconscious.

Charles Simic has been awarded a Pulitzer Prize and a MacArthur "genius" grant and generally has not wanted for recognition. But, despite giving ample evidence of his particular strengths, the *Selected Poems* doesn't quite make the case for putting Simic in the first class of contemporary poets. Simic's poetry may be deliberately limited, and this may be some of its strength and appeal, yet it is still limited. There is a type of pungent, image-rich lyric which Simic does supremely well. There are many types of poetry that Simic does either barely or not at all. It's an impression compounded by the decision to omit the prose poems and the longer sequence "White" from this collection. The constriction of tone, poetic techniques and musical effect, of subject matters and approach, whether in an individual poem or across the *oeuvre*, are as much marks of a minor poet as they are of a minimalist. Moreover, as Simic's career has progressed, his propensity to return to the same type of poem, the same images and ideas, has occasionally lapsed into the routine, while evidences of a more expansive, disquisitional, and overtly literary sensibility have been trapped in a style ill-suited to their expression. Nevertheless, there is much to be grateful for here. Simic's often humorous portrayal of life's pleasures (there are, for instance, few poets better on the subject of food) and his grasp upon some of its mysteries and terrors can be singular, potent, and rewarding.

WILLIAM WOOTTEN

Mouth to mouth

Radmila Lazić, *A Wake for the Living*, translated and with an introduction
by Charles Simic, Bloodaxe, £8.95, ISBN 1852246596

At first glance Radmila Lazić seems an unlikely candidate for translation by fellow-Serb Charles Simic, that anomalously Central European fabulist and ironist. *A Wake for the Living* introduces us to a predominantly first-person, violently confessional poetry of female experience, of sex and desire. In his Introduction, however, Simic offers her "uncommon eloquence … words that strike home" as the key to Lazić's work; and it's plain this is the common ground. A blunt, ringing clarity at its best generates images so compelling they seem undeniable: "My skin is velvet on the inside, / Like iris . […] /My body, so wintry a moment ago, / Is now a bush full of wild bees."

Some of the poems collected here could certainly count among the strongest in contemporary Balkan writing. "From my 'Kingdom'" is an *unheimlich* evocation of the landscape of solitude:

> The history of solitude is long.
> It's made up of a string of individuals
> That resemble each other like blades of grass […].
> I can turn and see the forest
> Walking after me step by step
> Like a sleepwalker in a dream.

Predictably, however, Lazić never allows such landscapes to over-grow her highly-charged processes of personification and sexualisation. In the subversive "Autumn Ode" she declares, "I'll celebrate October and not May, / The striptease of trees instead of orgasm of blossoms". (There's a similar euphony in the original.) This is serious wit, often rising to exuberance: "I don't want anyone to snore next to me / Like a choir of saws in a forest / While I drill the ceiling with my eyes all night long" ("The Bliss of Departure"). It deploys imagery with such ease that we don't even notice the virtuoso doubling of metaphor: "I'm no longer the little chrysanthemum / For you to scratch your balls with" ("Lyric Consequences"). An analogous irony characterises two of the most successful pieces in the book, the virtual elegy of "There, Here" and the literally elegiac "Last Voyage: New York-Belgrade", one of the few poems to situate itself in

a country
Whose citizens return
Like blind travellers
Without daydreams, without tears.
Like jars of hand cream
Or compacts in strangers' purses.

Lazić is indeed, as the book-cover proclaims, an activist: *Pro Femina*, the journal of which she was founding editor, does more than simply ensure that women writers and intellectuals get read in Serbia (problematic enough): it has changed the whole discursive landscape in Belgrade. She's also distinguished as part of the Belgrade Circle who, from the 1970s onwards, used scenes from urban life in a poetics of regime resistance. Lazić, who demonstrates in these poems the vivid complexity of her thinking, is nevertheless overwhelmingly represented here by pieces about the loss of love and need for sex. Among the best of these are the variegated splendours of the Freudian "A Woman's Letter": "With a belly up to my teeth, hands in the dough, / Face covered with flour, my heart a cinder / And his hand on my ass." Doubtless many readers can exclaim with recognition at passages like these; but the effect is sometimes repetitive, and there's just a whiff of the fashionable steering of a woman poet away from the Big Boys' table.

However, in this generously laid-out parallel-text edition, Bloodaxe once again introduce Anglophone readers to a new voice and, to some extent, a new poetics: we tend to know poets of the Serbian Banat (Vasko Popa, Ivan Lalić, Ioan Flora) better than the Belgrade Circle. This format also allows one to "read" both the extraordinary poets at work here, in a collection which destabilises and refreshes both language and experience. As Lazić declares (in "The Poems I Write"), "Words are embers. I burn myself into poetry."

FIONA SAMPSON

Turbulence in Russian souls

Tatiana Shcherbina, *Life Without: Selected Poetry and Prose 1992–2003*,
translated by Sasha Dugdale, Bloodaxe, £8.95, ISBN 1852246421

> Moscow: just those two syllables
> cause turbulence in Russian souls
> (Alexander Pushkin, *Eugene Onegin*)

At long last poetry translated into English is enjoying a revival. What is more, it is increasingly published in bilingual editions so that readers can at least gain the sound of the original (providing they acquaint themselves with the alphabet and basic rhythms of the original language). It seems that the British have decided that foreign languages are not all Greek to them.

Translated poetry opens up new directions for the poetry of its host language, and it may be significant that in the last year three women poets from different Slavonic languages have been published in Britain; Mila Haugová from Slovakia, Radmila Lazic from Serbia and Tatiana Shcherbina from Russia. All three write enormously dissimilar poetry thus offering a variety of strategies and procedures to British poetry. Tatiana Shcherbina's *Life Without* indicates how much poetic power can be generated by using established form and an associative technique of rapidly succeeding images:

> Life has caved in,
> has started to resemble a sine wave graph,
> a wearying numbness, a hunched back.

The subtitle "poetry and prose from 1992–2003", reinforced by Sasha Dugdale's introduction, concentrates the reader's attention on the 1990s when Russia underwent massive economic, social, and political change. Shcherbina's poetry is replete with the material detritus of this decade: whether from the Ebola virus or the Internet, the availability of cheese spread or the tacky illusions of the conjuror, David Copperfield.

However, although the 1990s may have been a unique decade in Russian history, it does not mean that the Russian poetry of this decade can be viewed as entirely different from what came before. Shcherbina's use of rhyme and metre shows that the central tradition of Russian poetry is as essential for her as it was for Joseph Brodsky. Her image-making with the proliferation of "kak" ("as" or "like") prompts comparison with the "kakophony" of early

Pasternak, another Muscovite, although Shcherbina is by and large an urban poet without Pasternak's abiding relationship with nature. Like a third Muscovite, Marina Tsvetayeva, she spent some years in Paris and, like Tsvetayeva, she felt compelled to return to Moscow, although, unlike Tsvetayeva, she enjoyed esteem for her work there and a life materially comfortable and rich in friendships. Shcherbina's poems do not lack the fierce emotions of Tsvetayeva's work, for example "The whole town is lit by my desire", although I would say that she has a greater gift of self-irony, a quality which does not completely come through in these translations. Irony prompts Shcherbina to mix classical reference with absolutely contemporary language. In "To Apollo" "God's answer phone is crap as well", and instead of formal prayer "I spray my request like an aerosol" before demanding "a classical turn of events, / where supplication meets with success".

In "Ru.net", one of the two poems which stretch beyond thirty lines, the past is present even if in the form of a disavowal: "neither Kostroma or Kamchatka survives" (alas, the grammatical solecism is the translator's, not a misprint), the former place being where Osip Mandelstam is believed to have perished and the latter the furthest eastern peninsula of the Soviet Union. Besides being a *tour de force* of image-making, this poem foregrounds the idea of the end of the largest nation state, the idea always having been false since the reality compelled a number of nationalities into the same totalitarian *laager*. Shcherbina is ambiguous about the new realities; she writes "Geographical might has fallen" and at the end of the poem "society falls away – the same society / in which we played the fool and played at war".

As well as stringing images together to expand a theme, Shcherbina is adept at extending a metaphor. "Pearl" and "Vicious Circle", next to each other in the selection, are wonderful examples. In "Pearl" she opens with the unexpected "A pearl is the barrenness of a shell" reversing the conventional technique of opening with an image of beauty then subsequently undercutting it. The beautiful images "lamplight in place of the soft pillow" and "mirrored light like a dog on guard" play catch up to the opening sally, but never entirely restore the received response. The disparity is never more evident than in the last verse where this time a beautiful image does begin the quatrain; "The pearl is the masterpiece of the river kingdom", but the response is even more devastating; "demons from the earth search for the shell / to sell its talent like a fairground charm / and destroy the oysters as they go".

"Vicious Circle" – despite the feebly translated first line, "Circle, you're horribly round" (I don't understand why Dugdale changes "vicious[ly]" to "horribly") – sustains and develops images of roundness and cicularity throughout the entire poem ending with a brilliant pun found in translation (it makes up for the first line); "and there you find hope – / there's a hoop and you're back in its grip".

This review would not do justice to Shcherbina's work if it failed to mention the love poems, which are complex, wry in feeling and packed full of imagery. A particular triumph (and in the translation, too, with its compensating consonance and assonance for the original rhymes) is "Life Without You":

> Life without you is neglected, ramshackle
> cheap and simply unapproachable,
> nightmarish like a provincial grocer's shack

At the end of the book is a selection of Shcherbina's short prose, but in translation only. As with her poems, a succession of thoughts and images flow out in rapid, but coherent fashion. Her humour is more evident and I find her less dogmatic than the impression given by Dugdale's introduction. Dugdale writes, "Russia's size and shifting borders make it impossible for her to know the country or feel anything for it: she is a Muscovite". But this has a different emphasis from Shcherbina's "I don't altogether understand what Russia is. It is too vast, too multilingual, too multicultural".

Dugdale has translated this excellent writer with great fidelity, and has achieved notable successes with a number of the poems, despite one or two slips. But these are to be expected when translating a poet so vital and complex in the original. *Life Without* is recommended to those who want to read a marvellous lyrical poet new to them and who want to know how a Russian poet feels in "the new world order".

JAMES SUTHERLAND-SMITH

Poems not photographs

Angus Reid, *White Medicine*,
Mariborska literarna druzba (Slovenia), ISBN 9616329960

Angus Reid lives and works in Slovenia; although you might not know that from reading *White Medicine*. Where contemporary Slovenian poetry is dominated by an expansive "Beat" poetics, its inclusivity stretched to the point of surrealism, Reid is hieratic. Where the Slovenians of his generation, from Iztok Osojnik to Peter Semolič, are urban, pacy, self-referential, Reid's "white medicine" is the "silence" of meditation, "the / foreground a crystal's / tangle of hangars" ("Untitled 22/365").

The crisp image could be a legacy of Martianism, or from the Stainer of *Paradise Island*. Reid, though, is heading off in quite another direction, out of what he calls the "lazy 8 / of infinity" into the movement of emotion. This sonnet moves, too, from the contemplated crystal to the conclusion that:

all headed together into
deep freezing darkness and
light was only there to be

we were
the same
the last of the
beautiful

This may sound like *anomie*, but Reid is anything but dismissive of experience. The poems in this book visit the concrete world with vivid attention:

In all things a whiteness
arising: metal in the milky
oyster prised apart for
medicine a shatterline
in splintered window
cutlery [...]

This unpunctuated listing throws together whitenesses so that they seem apparent everywhere; it also throws the relationships between medicine and broken glass, between window glass and the domestic clatter of cutlery, into relief. Such overt insertion of meaning into the world of experience makes for a risky poetics. For the most part, however, Reid pulls it off; often very well indeed. He's particularly good at endings which pose new possibilities, lifting easily into the proverbial ("and not to be feared, a future / in small things") or – on the "hell" of the Bosnian/Croatian border – the unexpected: "The border – // where the striplight / magnifies anybody's ecstasy". This is careful diction too: that "anybody" which replaces the expected "everybody" gives us the anonymity of border crossings, their precise lack of solidarity.

Reid is, in fact, a master technician. Two-thirds of this collection is given over to a sequence of syllabic sonnets with, as the author tells us, "fourteen lines of ten syllables each... with a regular "tear" into sections of ninety-eight and forty-two syllables. This allows the righthand section to be read as a commentary, summary, or a separate poem." Not only this, but what we have here are the first two crowns (each fifteenth sonnet is a "magistrale" of successive lines from the previous fourteen) from a proposed 365-sonnet sequence. This pressure-cooker of form produces, paradoxically, a decompressed, suggestive imagery, in which narrative is always just disappearing around the corner ahead of us:

I am still
I'm safe in the light   I do not know you

("Untitled 34/365")

Safe in the water-squat of   a green word
under that broken concrete   a thin man
is listening to the rain

("Untitled 1/365").

Personal and impersonal histories wait at the margins of these poems, from the lovers' row verging on existential conflict – "I'm leaving you / no I'm not leaving you   I'm leaving you" – to Slovenia's shifting Western border or Roman history. There are appearances by Romantic national poets (Prešeren, the founding father of Slovenian as a literary language, and Robert Burns); by Lavinia, Roman martyr; even by the poet's mother.

"These poems / are not photographs" but they do produce what Reid calls "chase-it-away shadow-play   images" ("Untitled 16/365"). Although one or two in the first section of the book are perhaps less accomplished (a stunning last line hardly redeems earlier uncertainties of register in Reid's version of the Hasan Aga ballad), Reid is an extremely interesting poet who deserves a wider readership.

FIONA SAMPSON

Half Zen, half Zeno

Rae Armantrout, Up to Speed,
Wesleyan University Press, $13.95, 0819566985

San Diego poet Rae Armantrout has been publishing for around 25 years. Her impressive selected poems, *Veil* (Wesleyan, 2001), provided an overview of some of the continuities in her work: juxtapositions of register, gnomic wit, compressed paradox and a preoccupation with temporality. She often roots her poetry in material drawn from her own day-to-day experience. Overheard conversations, pop-culture gobbets and events seen from her window leak into her poems and suddenly become very strange. She has developed a style that is oriented, from top to bottom, around minutely judged explorations of states of uncertainty. *Up to Speed*, Armantrout's first book since *Veil*, shows her becoming increasingly interested in the not-so-simple question of how one thing follows another in poems.

Again and again when reading this work, one returns to the suggestion, in "Exceptional", that "there *are* no / sequences".

Armantrout's poems tend to be short and her use of the short line is the most salient aspect of her technique. Her "voice", if it is located anywhere, finds itself in the pauses between her lines. Unlike many of her peers (she is associated with the West Coast language poetry scene), she is not a poet of syntactical rupture. When the line breaks, a few words into one of her enjambed sentences, there's a miniature glitch in its movement. In such short-line work, these momentary suspensions of sequence have a cumulative effect, strewing her paths of thought with pot-holes. Armantrout uses this braking technique to caution against the ways in which we unthinkingly allow the forward-moving sentence to fix us in time – how we tend to collude with authors in assenting to the temporal schemes they draw us into.

The poems of *Up to Speed* often return to the difficulty of isolating the present moment. A voice in one poem, "En Route", worries that "we're always / 'about to' or / 'have just'." Another, in "Box", speculates about: "A time when we agree // the present does not exist, // has never existed". The repeated stab of the line-break is a means of building these equivocal perceptions about time and the present into the formal texture of Armantrout's work. The physical breaks on the page cause thought to turn back on itself, confronting the reader with the nagging intrusion of a present moment that is past as soon as one begins to think about it.

There are many apparently simple statements that use the verb "to be" in these poems. Such formulations tend to undo themselves at the moment of utterance – the word "is" buckles in the heat of Armantrout's aphoristic for-mulations and becomes another way of saying "is not". Examples might be: "(A thought / is a wish for relation / doubling as a boundary.)"; "the opposite of nothingness // is direction"; "a maternal hand / is lavender-suffusing / dusk"; "Some say / matter's really energy // and energy is force / of law // and law is just / tautology." The bluntest form of statement – that something *is* this or that – dissolves into equivocation.

This anxiety about the possibility of making even simple statements also surfaces in the kinds of direct question that Armantrout asks in her poems. Half Zen, half Zeno, such questions as "Does a road / run its whole length / at once?" or "what is a collision?" bring a close focus to bear on the relationship of parts to wholes within temporal sequences. One way of sifting this querying of sequence into the poetry is by writing grammatically-intact sentences that refuse to add up. The sudden change of direction – what critic Hank Lazer has called Armantrout's "lyricism of the swerve" – trips up the habitual step-by-step gait of the reader. The following three lines open "Upper World": "If sadness / is akin to patience, // we're back!"

The sombre opening slips into cheery bathos with the sudden tonal shift of "we're back!" The play of registers becomes clearer later in the poem, as it moves from "every name's Eurydice, / briefly returned from blankness" to "High voices / over rapid-pulsing synthesizers / intone, 'without you' – // which is soothing." As motifs of absence and mythic loss accumulate, the virtue of patience is stranded somewhere between a Penelope-like fortitude and the commodification of feeling in music. The entire poem, one of the densest in the collection, grows out of the significance that the swerve in the first three lines retrospectively accumulates.

There's another level of sequential disarrangement besides that of line and sentence. Armantrout's poems are (increasingly so in recent years) often mini-series composed of tangentially related units. (George Oppen's "Discrete Series", the title culled from mathematics, comes to mind as a descriptive term.) Once again, ordinary forward progress is stymied. The various sections qualify and take issue with one another in unpredictable ways, acknowledging that they are part of a larger whole but insisting on their own singularity. Armantrout's handling of series builds a larger-scale hesitation into the work, allowing for complex perspectival effects that cause the poems almost to reconstitute themselves with each successive visit.

The curious language of tabloid-style journalism is a resource that is often plundered for the riddles and speculative chasms that open in the texts. "Boy Wins Love With Tall Tale", for example, sits, in all its exhilarating oddness, at the head of one poem, "Visualisations". As the poem develops over its two sections, filaments of sense connect the apparently disconnected. The poem wonders about truth-telling and belief, slowly unpicking itself to reveal a reservoir of doubt about the possibility of either. It concludes with another headline, "Umbilical Stump Still Pulses", which combines horror-film schlock with an echo of the tale/tail that opened the poem. The pulsing stump might even be one of the outcomes of the love announced in the first line. This scrupulously laconic wit is one of Armantrout's great strengths. Her amused play with incongruity and ellipsis works to extend the reach of the questions about language and culture that her verse is asking – she has spoken of the way her poetry monitors the "interventions of capitalism into consciousness". The messages of contemporary American culture are scrambled by the energy and wit of Armantrout's rapid re-edits. Her verse is more than up to that culture's speed, leaving it wrapped in its own self-absorption, as this telegaphic sci-fi summary suggests: "In the shorter version, // tentacled / stomach swallows stomach."

WILL MONTGOMERY

Sunny side up

Anthony Caleshu *The Siege of the Body and A Brief Respite*,
Salt, £9.95, ISBN 1844710173

nthony Caleshu is an American, a native of Massachusetts who for a
time lived in Boston. Since 1997 he has lived and worked in Ireland and
England. His play *In the Bedroom* has been produced, and *The Siege of
the Body and a Brief Respite* is his first book of poems.

It is a book with an overall design into which stand-alone poems have
been fitted. It is both an unconventional book with alternating sections "The
Siege of the Body", "A Brief Respite", and a conventional one of poems written
as necessity and inspiration demanded. Caleshu wants it both ways, which is a
risk work taking. In my view, he is a better, more satisfying poet than the
design of this book allows him to be. There is a shorter, more coherent and
readable book, perhaps an 80 page book, in these 120 pages.

The best poems, which make up the book's love story, are in the three
"The Siege of the Body" sections. The two "And a Brief Respite" sections, the
first titled "(Dialogues)" and the second "(Collaborations)" are simply not
believable. I hear not two voices but one arranged into two, and I have no idea
who the collaborators are. Caleshu writes a suave long line: "– Into this
woman's headpiece of turquoise feathers / I am whispering everything
unimaginable." Reading these sections is like watching figure skating on
television. There is skill at work, but I could not get beyond my disbelief at the
convention and felt throughout like a slightly bored spectator.

When I decided not to follow the design of this book but to open it at
random I discovered a live and appealing poet. "Love, I have Spent in that
House" (Caleshu peppers his book with quotes from writers as disparate as
David Hume, Lou Reed and George Oppen – "Love, I have Spent..." is a James
Dickey line) is a terrific poem, rollicking and funny, built on a William Carlos
Williamsish three step "variable foot" stanza. The poem picks you up and
doesn't let go:

> The sun's ultimatum
> > Through the bedroom blinds
> > > Live and Love

> Or stay in bed forever
> > Curled into no one
> > > The sort of attack a child has

Whose mother has gone to the store
        I check your jewellery drawer
                For anything missing

I should ask you now
        Before you go missing
                We should you know

Get married
        I'll follow you to your research
                We'll buy a house

A home
        In the country like you want
                In Maine

Where you'll have more lobsters for study
        And we'll have more days of snow
                No matter

I love the snow
        I can practice my skiing I can—
                And I am down these old stairs

Bounding
        The rambling nun of the streets
                Looking for you

This is a poem of masculine anxiety and the domestic comfort – breakfast eggs, melon and toast – that can soothe it. The poem has a subject and holds its focus. Its artful lines communicate the jitters. There are other good poems in this book, but "Love, I have Spent in that House" is the one I have bookmarked.

    This is a first book from which I can imagine nothing of the poet's future. Caleshu may well come to see that in the "Respite" sections, idea trumps execution and will steer clear of such ideas in the future. Or he may see that, in poetry, ideas are useful but (as Mallarmé said to his friend Degas) secondary to words. Well, for all the many times the word "promise" has been used, a poet's first book is not a crystal ball. It is the here and now that matters. Caleshu's book ends with a lovely, melancholy poem of joint self-knowledge.

One voice says "– Remind me how you used to float above me …" And the other answers, "like a cloud of mistakes over time". It strikes me as exactly the right note for this book to end on.

WILLIAM CORBETT

Body building

Michael Symons Roberts, *Corpus*,
Jonathan Cape, £8.00, ISBN 0224073427

If someone were to write a book about poetry in Britain and Ireland since the war, and to centre it on the theme of dead bodies, they could easily take in some of the most influential poems of the period, including Keith Douglas's "How to Kill", Ted Hughes's "View of a Pig" and Seamus Heaney's "The Grauballe Man". Further significant examples could be admitted from the poetry of Michael Longley, Paul Muldoon, John Burnside, Ian Duhig and Robin Robertson, and somewhere along the line the writer might want to look at *Corpus* by Michael Symons Roberts, a book which owes a lot to this minor tradition and which, at the same time, mildly extends it.

Perhaps the principal reason for the prevalence of "corpse-poetry" since the war is the handy way such poems let us sort through moth-eaten metaphysical dualisms like "soul" and "body", and to see how they hold up – if they hold up at all – in our post-Darwinian, post-Lawrentian world of globalisation and genetic technology. As Heaney put it when contemplating an Iron Age ancestor: "Who will say 'corpse' / To his vivid cast? / Who will say 'body' / To his opaque repose?" Well, Michael Symons Roberts might.

In a poem which occurs early in the book, the speaker imagines himself as a dead body. The emotional interest of the poem lies in what the reader wants, or needs, to make of the spectacle:

Back street. No cars. Men step
over me, dogs and crows investigate.

My eyes gape. Circuitry of soul
is broken. I am in an odd shape

– twisted star – a pose I could never
strike in life. Gymnastic, almost.

Symons Roberts is careful not to manipulate our reactions too much. At most we are offered minor cues – a word like "circuitry", even when used with a word like "soul", invites us to read the scene in physicalist terms, to conclude there is nothing more than atoms here. A word like "star", on the other hand, invites us to read the same scene in metaphysical terms. The suspension between these possibilities is the central motif of the book.

In this and other necrophagous passages, the narcotic tone is appropriate but a little monotonous. Symons Roberts is a careful, rather than spectacular, poet. His greatest strength is his ability to come up with original ideas for poems, and it is those ideas, rather than particular lines or phrases, which tend to stay in the mind: for example, that stars don't move but the space between them does, that the Earth is a creature which has been skinned, that we dream of mermaids because we evolved from the sea. The rhythms of the book are limited in scope – there is scarcely a line with more than five beats, or a stanza with more than five lines. This limited technical palette, however, allows us to focus on Symons Roberts's other main virtues: imagery, diction, and psychological acuity. He has been a documentary film-maker – and often the poems come across like scripts with brisk directions.

In his poem "The Box", which has parallels with a similarly-titled poem by Hans Magnus Enzenberger, Symons Roberts imagines a box which would hold items – a leaf, a child's hair – from which humanity and the world could be reconstructed. The poem concludes: "Spores, antennae, claws, / the box will hold all evolution. / It will be full and empty." The paradox of the conclusion points to the ambiguous value of the world around us. Does it have a value, other than the values we choose to attribute to it? A consistent and thoughtful book, which is well worth reading, *Corpus* asks difficult questions of us.

JOHN REDMOND

Close to home

Susan Wicks, *Night Toad: New and Selected Poems*,
Bloodaxe, £8.95, ISBN 185224637

I'm ashamed to admit it, but Susan Wicks's poetry seems to have rather passed me by over the years. So while *Night Toad: New and Selected Poems* offers, for this reader at any rate, a long overdue introduction to the breadth of Wicks's style and preoccupations, it remains primarily just that: an introduction. It's arguably a troubling sign of the times, and of crushing market forces, that just a little over a decade's work becomes premature occasion for refinement and retrospective, if only, it would seem, to keep the older poems in print and provide a platform for the new.

But *Night Toad* does, indeed, prove in the main a most welcome read, even if there are few fireworks on offer and the material that Wicks fashions is simple and often slight. Wicks is a domestic-oriented poet, with a neat line in defining, or perhaps more precisely elevating, the extraordinary in the resolutely mundane. Unsurprisingly, this makes for something of a mixed bag.

Despite the modesty and reservation of her tone and style, Wicks is a poet in the confessional vein. She is at her very best when working close to the bone and close to home, detailing her relationships with her parents, for example, or presenting the negotiation of a lifetime of loves lost and found, with a variously clinical and vulnerable expertise. This approach allows her writing to develop in touching and often intimate directions. In a fine piece such as "Weir", for instance, where I suspect the pun in the title is fully intended, memory, time and love seem at once to fail and to overcome the subject, as meditations on mortality shade and lighten (literally and figuratively) the world:

> In moving water
> our world is precious as wreckage,
> its sunken carcass rolled and
> remade; the impact of a drop
> rings us like deep treasure.
>
> This is where time slides open
> on a sheet of sky, as the churned bodies
> of trunks rise for ever, bare
> a gleam of white shoulders.

Although here, as in many of Wicks's poems, I'm occasionally unconvinced by the arbitrariness of Wicks's line-breaks, I found this a satisfying and emotive offering, and companion pieces, such as "Mute Swans", "My Father's Handkerchiefs" and "Forgotten Light", illuminate her often wise and unfashionably earnest talent for elegy. Certainly, *The Clever Daughter* (1996), from which these particular poems have been selected, and which garnered for Wicks much acclaim, seems to hold, to my mind at any rate, much of the standout material collected here.

For despite the undeniable successes, I couldn't shake the feeling that a fair number of poems felt, despite their attribution and appeal to the ordinary, forced or "faked" in their mode of address and, indeed, in what they purported to say or not say about the world. Poems from the new collection, *Night Toad*, seemed to me to be bordering dangerously on the workshop exercise, with such inclusions as "Optician" (admittedly a commission), "Walkman", "Contact" and an inexplicably bizarre response to Von Trier's cinematic mini-masterpiece *Breaking the Waves* called, well, "Breaking the Waves" doing lamentably poor justice indeed to Wicks's skill and ruminative mind.

That said, *Night Toad* is a refreshing and happily unpretentious and unposturing accumulation of work; making no great claims, it stakes none either. Whether you love or hate the approach, or feel generally indifferent to it, Wicks subtly demonstrates – and to her credit – the value of turning down the artistic volume a notch, if only to ensure the reader can hear him or herself think.

KATHRYN GRAY

First-time buyer

Kathryn Gray, *The Never-Never*, Seren, £7.99, ISBN 1854113658

There is something awfully familiar about Kathryn Gray's *The Never-Never*. While it may be unfair to foist descriptive categories upon a first collection, to read these competent lyrics is to be reminded that every generation has its own form of poetic diction, a notion that did not, in fact, expire with Thomas Gray and the eighteenth century. Gray (Kathryn) name-checks some of the contemporary practitioners of this art in her acknowledgements, so one has a fair idea of what to expect. And sure enough, all of the usual features are there: the ironised, eye-level take on estate life, joyriding, blokeishness, booze and fags, sex in cheap B&Bs, all laced with just enough clever allusion and formal zest to pack that necessary millennial punch.

Kathryn Gray proves she can be as blokeish as the best of them. There is no danger of sentimentality (proximity to which must be avoided at all costs) in "The Muse, An Estate", where an equivalence is drawn between the poet's urge to write, and her orientation of herself inside a landscape which would seem inimical: "Closed and unleverable as that / scratched-out, tagged steel / of the month-long broken lifts, in a birl of drum and bass / (just to *keep it real*)". Nights out with the girls are eulogised in "Where Did Our Love Go?" and "Friend", in which two drunken girls find themselves "miles from morning doorsteps, / two women on an A-road and we stop to explain to one another ... / please be quiet, come nearer and let our cupped hands / pool the languages of loose change, mascara, fiver". In poems like these Gray nails her colours to the mast, but the problem with sentimentality is that if it is not risked then the poem can entirely lose emotional register.

There is exuberance and formal relish in some poems here, but Gray's subjects and angle of approach, because of and not despite being disabused – "deconsecrated" as Maurice Riordan puts it – are in danger of seeming conventional. The by-now familiar disjunction between subject (see above) and elliptical style occasionally forces her into laboured abstraction and swollen phrasing. This, from "Garage", is the second of three very long sentences of which the poem is composed:

Here, simple Dulux,
petrified in a virgin tin, holds the sum untried hope
of newlywed, first-time buyers and, in the box,
merely happened upon, a loose swatch of Anaglypta
is a lounge, as was, a decade gone, whose print I read,
like the tabloid around that lampshade, as a *then* politics;
while, against brick, the Raleigh outgrows again stabilisers
and its pedals recall a girl in a *no hands* freewheeling
along some slope of road.

There must be half a dozen unnecessary words in this extract alone. However she puts this tendency to good satirical use in "You Hated Your Flat", a poem which is funny because it sends up Ted Hughes's own egotistical disparities between subject-matter and style.

The dense texture of Gray's writing tends to slow the eye, sometimes to genuinely striking effect, as in "The Singularity" which is a lovely and mysterious poem: "Perfectly round and beyond this, something grew – as if planned for – / even as a cultured pearl and, more, simply kept growing there,

/ until each of our days fell into one another and the space fell out". This poem demonstrates what Gray is capable of when she writes in an unforced way.

CAITRIONA O'REILLY

Shedding light

Gillian Allnutt, *Sojourner*, Bloodaxe Books, £7.95 ISBN 1852246693

The poems in *Sojourner* are spare, often consisting of one stuttering, half-retrieved line. It is a relief to read poems unafraid to declare inadequacy, to pay homage to the superiority of silence, as here, from "The Widow's Mite: Effie, Dumfries, August 1916":

> Bring out the boots that will no longer need to be repaired.

> Bring them to the bare hillside.

> Lovely is the harebell.
> Still, frail.

The apparent redundancy of the boots and the verbose "will no longer need to be repaired" is resolved by the rhyming echoes of "bare hillside" and "harebell".

The spirit of the whole collection lives in the glorious last line of "'The Old Town Hall and St Hilda's Church, Middlesborough' by L.S. Lowry": "Or they were born yesterday and do not know that during the war." This incomplete sentence *is* complete, fully meriting its full-stop. To continue would be to say too much. All Allnutt's poems are like that, complete fragments, many of them only four or six lines long. Typical images are of incompletion – missing an oar ("Black Madonna") or even "half an oar" ("The Little Cello, Gydnia, 1949").

Logical connections, likewise, have been laid aside, and replaced by rhythm, repetition and rhyme: "How the bicycle shone" begins each line with "and how"; and in "Winter Interior", from the sequence "A Shepherd's Life: *Paintings of Jenny Armstrong by Victoria Crowe*", the sound and sense of "winter" echo through the poem:

Sheep in smirr

Without shadow now, the snow,
the straw strewn by her.

She reads indoors.

Words grow smaller.

The kettle on the stool waits with her
through winter.

The open vowel in "war" caws through the whole of "In Miss Macauley's Class": "we wear the great war of the world", "Our words", "We're part of the hoard", "crowd", "war-gear".

The shortest poem, "The Fifties", conjures up both the deprivation and promise of that post-war decade ("There were windows the war had left alone. / Imagine. / A world that would open"), while the previous poem, "Literature in Childhood" makes do – "All the time, outside literature, fear was going on. // There were sandwiches, Marmite usually, Spam" – and the last image of "Puppet" leads to coming horrors: "I was laid aside, like Czechoslovakia. // My strings were made of raw silk, red, and rotted / at sea and knotted themselves around me."

The brevity of the *Sojourner* poems, though singly striking, does have the effect of rendering the collection a little thin and unbalanced, as if it might just blow away, perhaps aptly, since it devotes itself to the voices and memories of the unheard, the anonymous, the forgotten. Some of the northern places and names are left unexplained, whilst others are over-referenced in over-long titles and notes. "German Woman, 1945" includes the word "marching" – there is clearly no need for the note "*Soldaten*: soldiers". "From the Artist's Notebook: / *After some paintings of girls and women / by Paula Modersohn-Becker*" is followed by thirteen lines of notes.

The poems deserve more silence, more space. They work far better than notes as illumination for each other and themselves. The very first poem, entitled "To a Last" and addressed to a cobbler's last, is balanced by the last poems that celebrate a girl's rite of passage into womanhood: first things are placed last, the last placed first. Allnutt's own tact and delicacy shed more light than any explanatory note or title.

JUDY KENDALL

Chance encounter

Kona Macphee, *Tails*, Bloodaxe, £7.95, ISBN 185224660X

As the title suggests, *Tails* deliberates on the kind of chance evident in a coin toss. Such Hardyesque fatefulness provides a guiding principle for many poems in the collection. In the face of fate, the act of interpretation can be a way of trying to force its hand rather than accepting it, and, implicitly recognising this, the best poems in *Tails* value observation over explicit interpretation, manifesting a humane disinterest. This is to say, Kona Macphee's finest work presents a perspective whose detachment is rooted in genuine care for what it sees, as though the refusal to centre the poems in a personal subjectivity will provide the most intimate connection to the world. Add to this meticulous attention a lyricism based on compressed syntax and skilful consonance, and the result is such poems as "Terminus", which concludes:

> Perspective's engine hauls the eyes
> along the single-gauge, the groove
> of jumbling rocks, which slant toward
> a station hidden past the sliced
> horizon. Here, no train to board.
> The hot air shimmers. Nothing moves.

The "perspective's engine" in *Tails* arises, in part, from the first three poems' use of three different points of view (second, first, and third person, respectively), which initially establishes a detachment between the poet and the speaker that continues, for a time, in the succeeding poems. This standpoint is further enhanced by the interspersing of personal narrative among other types of poem, as we meet accounts of the nonhuman world, historical situations, and a surreal dream, so that when "Waltz" gives a third-person close-up of two dancers, the interest lies in the way a sort of physics informs the physical such that the poem, in spite of its subject, resists sentimentality.

As the foregoing suggests, *Tails* offers an impressive range, indicative of a mature first collection. Many poetry volumes' blurbs herald the great variety of their contents, but often the report proves untrue in the experience of reading the books themselves. Sometimes this happens because the descriptions exaggerate, but more often the narrowness of the poems' approach diminishes an array of topics to simplified and similar themes and arguments, so that the poems themselves seem very alike despite their superficially diverse subjects. *Tails*, on the contrary, lives up to its advertisement and more, for its variety extends beyond mere topics to perspectives and forms: from the more associative, double-spaced lines of "Shrew", to the villanelle "A Prayer", to the aphoristic "Scales", to the lighthearted "Yode", where a saying of the *Star Wars* character Yoda serves as the last line of each of its four quatrains.

The book does not, unfortunately, consistently maintain the productive disinterest that generates its strong beginning. Apparently autobiographical poems about romantic relationships and parenthood still offer the musicality found elsewhere, but here the poems' progressions and denouements become predictable, pat, sentimental. In "Birthday in a New House", for example, the speaker, addressing her partner, points out her crow's feet "that measure time in decades" and concludes:

> We will not fear
>
> these lines that spread the messages of age
> through lath and plaster, hair and skin; we know
>
> that no house stands forever, but that love
> can hold a house together long enough.

Juxtaposed with the ambitious work in the collection, "Birthday" appears all too easy: the speaker as a house, their signs of age, and the love that will sustain both. This poem, and a handful of others, fall noticeably short of the standard presented in "Cosmology 101" and "Taking Her In". It is with poems such as these that *Tails* impresses and raises hopes for further successes in Macphee's next volume.

CARRIE ETTER

Warhol in Wheatlands

John Kinsella, *Peripheral Light: Selected and New Poems*,
selected with an Introduction by Harold Bloom, Norton, £15.95,
ISBN 0393058212, *Lightning Tree*, Arc, £8.95, ISBN 1900072610
Outside the Panopticon, Prest Roots Press, £9, ISBN 1871237211

"The pastoral and the political possibilities of poetry", "Spatial rela-tionships", "A Brief Poetics" – these are the titles of some articles by John Kinsella, born in 1963, brought up in Australia and living now in Cambridge, England. They can be found on his website www.johnkinsella.org. Already Kinsella has over twenty-five books to his name. Of these most are poetry collections, with some fiction and drama. There are no books either of theory or research but Kinsella's short articles, expressed in an easy-going prose, signal an interest in a poetry of hybrids, and a poetry that mixes traditional forms and personal and local histories with the experimental techniques of the Language poets. A further cross is added, if needed, in the form of various affirmations of equality in gender difference, the rights of indigenous peoples especially in relation to land ownership, and the sanctity of animal life. Serious issues one and all, although readers who prefer more conventional narratives and evocative description may be reassured to find that Kinsella's poetry, despite his respect for syntactic obliquity, is relatively conventional. Others, seeking the more experimental approach, will find it occasionally to be against the grain of the poet's apparently mild and genial sensibility.

The rural remembrances and the explicit didacticism in Les Murray and Seamus Heaney's poetry are the better point of comparison here. When there are explicit Anglo-American–Australian cross-overs, as with the poems in which David Hockney's "Doll Boy" and Andy Warhol himself appear in the small Australian community of Wheatlands, a poetry of gentle comedy ensues rather like a fleshed out version of Robert Crawford's Einstein-in-Scotland squibs.

Many of Kinsella's poems are so relaxed formally – with individual lines and line-breaks nearly aurally and semantically freightless, whether framed in traditional form or not – it is difficult to see why a prose-poem form (which would still be a loose prose-poem form) was not chosen for many. Of the political issues, the theme of guardianship of the land is the only one that seethes again and again through Kinsella's body of work, and is absorbed so thoroughly that it, perhaps alone, manages not to foreground itself as a module in the first semester. In these rural poems there is the power not just of understatement but of situations which are ambiguous and unresolved, and whose quality resides in the unglossed openness of the initially mysterious.

Kinsella's poems of fertile landscapes salted up by white man's brutal ignorance, and of the same settler/occupiers themselves caught up in the tragedy of that fight with the land, unfold without the internal explanations that damage so many of the other pieces. Though they may heavily imply a moral lesson, the descriptions are rich and the telling either suspenseful or pleasurably oblique. The poet is right to assert, in his prose pieces, that the pastoral has considerable life in it yet, considerable bite even, and his own work in this mode is what makes him so worth re-reading.

For much of the rest, if this was art, the artist would not only be painting the picture and writing the exhibition catalogue, they would be photocopying bits of the catalogue and pasting the texts on to the paintings themselves. Kinsella's explanations do not have what could be taken as structurally self-conscious wit, however, and it is difficult to read lines like "But maybe now / we can see that such assumptions / were merely a matter of taste" (on once preferring America to the Soviet Union in the space race) as anything but well-intentioned educationalese, a peculiar loose and clichéd tone for a poem publically addressed to J. H. Prynne.

This problem of over-earnestness as a function of stylistic weakness is better handled in the series of "Poems on Linguistic Disobedience" where Language poetry's flotsamic energy places the poet's own helpful but banal analyses under the pressure of deconstruction. The poems within the beautifully printed *Lightning Tree* and *Outside the Panopticon* suggest that Kinsella is still at his best and worst on this score, as if his attention is always going to be divided between saying something and then contextualising it (and thus also pre-empting other contextualisations). An analytical discourse, though, can still have power if it's integrated, and control can be regained over a profligate poetry that seems often not in command of its own generative velocities. Kinsella need only look at his own earlier work to re-learn this.

RICHARD PRICE

Tabloid fantasia

August Kleinzahler, *The Strange Hours Travelers Keep*, Faber, £9.99,
ISBN 0571221734

August Kleinzahler's ludic, unpredictable poems map an America both real and imagined – or rather, reimagined through his idiosyncratic vision as a place where "pork bellies" jostle with "Unisys A-15 J mainframes" for significance, and where a bus garage morphs (via Hermann Hesse's *Siddhartha*) into a quasi-Buddhist "Cave of Illumination and Fumes". These snapshots of Kleinzahler's native land are sharply contemporary, as in a sonnet composed of what appear to be tabloid headlines ("BURGLARS TAKE GUILLOTINE AND HITLER'S PIANO / DISNEY HIRES KISSINGER"). The piece neatly skewers the Jerry Springer-style sensationalism that is one of America's most popular exports, while at the same time revelling in the genre's very exuberance and absurdity. A similar collage poem, the aptly named " 'Lil' Bits: American Foundlings", juxtaposes cryptic shop signs and fragments of overheard speech to create a suggestive "COCKTAIL" about the country's ruling obsessions: sex, money and instant gratification ("ROOT HOG OR LOSE YOUR ACORN").

Kleinzahler has a knack for collages and lists ("Food trucks, propane, tortured hearts"), forms suited to the randomness and multiplicity of (post-) modern existence. One suspects he also likes them because they generate meaning and ambiguity in equal measure – in a typical Kleinzahler piece, it's impossible to tell what the author's message is, what point he's making (or if, indeed, he's making a point at all). Though his strategy is refreshingly nonreductive, allowing him to sidestep the identity politics that infuse a certain strain of contemporary US poetry, sometimes he can be so oblique that the reader is simply left in the dark. Prime example: the baffling sequence "A History of Western Music", six poems purporting to be chapters of a book of the same title, scattered out of order through the collection (i.e., Chapter 4 comes after Chapter 11). They deliberately resist the expectations set up by their title – instead of a sober account of music history, we get a chaotic travelogue that name-checks Florence, Paris, Antwerp, and Frankfurt; alludes to figures like Mahler, Liberace, and Sarah Vaughn; and incorporates possibly spurious personal anecdotes. The register jumps from the jokey ("wife Alma was a troublesome slut") to the profane (references to fucking, cunts, cocks), along the way touching on the power of art and the subjectiveness of critics and audiences. The sequence amounts to a sort of *ars poetica*: of a fictional harpsichord virtuoso, Kleinzahler writes, "[He] put a prism over this world, in order to color it with his playing, visiting any one place only so long as the reverberation of a single plucked string". Likewise, Kleinzahler's method is to colour our world with his linguistic play, filtering everything through the prism of his restless, irreverent intelligence.

With his chatty, colloquial voice ("Rosy-fingered dawn, my ass") and feckless not-quite-narratives, Kleinzahler sounds like a Californian Frank O'Hara, *sans* winsomeness; the poems skitter away from anything that might be construed as pretentious in their diction, prosody, and subject matter. In this, as in their air of semi-intellectual japery, they also resemble John Ashbery's work. Kleinzahler's most compelling pieces, however, take a different tack – shorter, more lucid and direct in approach, they verge on traditional lyricism, but are no less original for that. The love poems "Across the Land" and "The Visit" admit wistfulness, nostalgia, heartache, and even slant rhyme into the picture, while "The Installation" conjures a piercingly real sense of claustrophobia from the author's visit to a waxwork-filled gallery. The ghastly, uncanny aura ("one can hardly breathe") builds to a conclusion that offers no release: "It is impossible to leave[.]" In these tightly controlled vignettes, Kleinzahler finds material worthy of his art.

JANE YEH

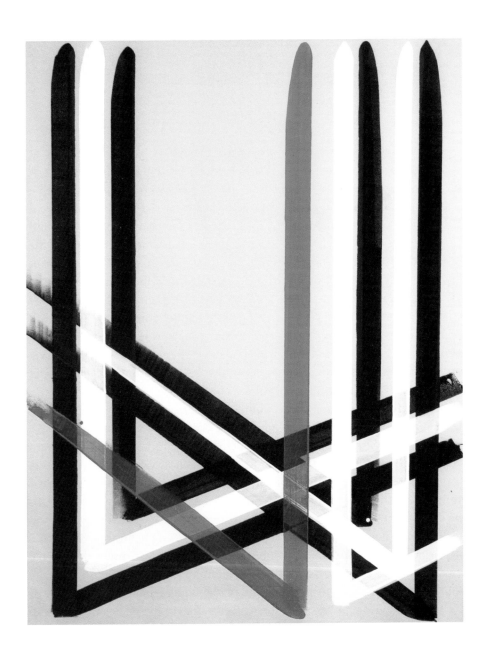

Poet in the Gallery

STEPHEN KNIGHT

Michael Landy, "Semi-detached"
27 May – 12 December 2004
Tate Britain

Placing a semi-detached house carbuncled with pebbledash and UPVC at the heart of the grandiose Tate Britain is a witty piece of devilment. A replica of the Essex home of the artist's parents, the house takes up a surprising amount of space; the chimney reaches for the vaulted ceiling, and there is little more than a pram's-width between the pointed brickwork and the gallery walls on either side. It is a startling achievement, a tribute to the team that constructed it under Michael Landy's direction: the TV aerial snakes down the wall, entering the house through an air-brick; the paintwork is deteriorating; a Neighbourhood Watch sticker peeps through the downstairs bay window; a biro is visible on a sill at the back; the net curtains are tired from too little, or to much washing. If art can make you consider the unconsidered, then Landy's house does so simply by a change of context. Who would have thought a pebbledashed wall could be so inviting to the touch, a letterbox at ankle height so fascinating?

Left at that, "Semi-detached" would be an intriguingly elliptical work: a bit of post-modern agitprop swiping at the class divide, Rachel Whiteread's eerie "House" with knobs on, or something to bracket with Duchamp's autographed urinal. But Michael Landy's semi is not only detached from its next-door neighbour, it is also bisected lengthwise, the two halves separated from one another and located about fifty paces apart. Three films projected on the cross-sections revealed as you walk around the façade are the meat of the installation. They wipe the smile off your face. Showing behind the front half of the house is "Four Walls", a montage of illustrations drawn from DIY manuals owned by the artist's father. The lighting is ghostly to allow the half-hour's worth of footage to register, though it also gives the space even more of the air of a mausoleum, an atmosphere well suited to the work's elegiac tone. To the melancholy soundtrack of a whistling man - whistling while he works, I guess – which echoes through the gallery so convincingly that I thought there was a Tate employee, just out of sight, angling for a dismissal, Landy has cut together images in which hands are an insistent motif; hands holding saws or scrapers or a pair of shears, hands repairing damaged plaster, blocked guttering, a corrugated roof, a rotten sill. (Watching a montage of stills is oddly unsettling. I was reminded of the sequence comprising Dust Bowl poverty, Vietnam GIs and Marvel Comics heroes shown to brainwash Warren Beatty's journalist in Alan J. Pakula's *The Parallax View*.) In Landy's film, everything is leaking, peeling or cracked; disrepair and decay are scarcely ameliorated by the busy hands. Landy lingers for a moment on a piece of damage before proceeding with rapid cuts, from hands and tools to drawings and photographs of men and women at work, people who might have been in their prime at any time between the 1950s and the 1970s. The superannuated illustrations are, of course, significant; this is Sisyphean work, and the outside of Landy's house attests to a losing battle.

The man who has already lost the battle is the artist's father. The victim of an industrial accident in 1977, housebound Mr Landy is, in fact, the subject of his son's installation, although there is nothing more of the man himself on the far wall, fifty paces away, than a hand, his feet, and possibly a few photographs. The installation's title is as much a reference to its cool scrutiny of Dad through the detritus of his life – his medication, his tools, the family snaps – as to the building itself.

There are two films showing on the other wall, "No. 62" and "Shelf Life". Pushing fifty minutes, the latter pans funereally over objects and photographs. It is a forensic inspection which begins with a Labour Party circular, its rose logo prominent, then moves across tools and manuals, a crusty Tipp-Ex bottle, sets of instructions and video cassettes, taking in, at regular intervals, wallpaper with a flower-like pattern. (Roses are another of the work's motifs.) In the absence of information about the photographs, we speculate. Is that Michael Landy as a child? Is the white-bearded man his father? To what or whom are the group at the pub-table giving the thumbs-up? From the speakers come faint birdsong and a sinister, mechanical rumble familiar from David Lynch films such as *Eraserhead* and *The Elephant Man*. Claustrophobic, bleak, the effect may be meant to mirror the plight of Landy's invalid father. This is, at any rate, no laughing matter.

Just over twenty minutes long, "No. 62" combines still and moving images, opening with the buzz of electricity and a light flickering on. The sequence that follows returns to an ashtray, shot from below, into which more and more cigarette ash is tapped while people chatter and a radio plays. "Semi-detached" is a work built of echoes, so the ashtray's glass-bubble design returns as the bubbling foot-spa in which we glimpse a pair of feet. Spinning in a breeze, a crucifix-shaped sliver of wood hangs from the ceiling of a garden shed, while, in another section, similarly suspended fluff vibrates in a draught. Then some blatant *mementos mori*: a dragonfly tits-up in a Tupperware container, a dead spider hanging upside down, a moth crushed against the wallpaper. A bedside table is cluttered with medication and a card

TO MY BEST GRANDAD . . . This really is no laughing matter.

The key image to which "No. 62" returns is, inevitably, a hand; its fingernails long and curved, its skin disconcertingly smooth. The hand – Mr Landy's, we assume – is first seen at rest, a still image that slowly comes to life. Later, it clutches at thin air as if its owner were in the act of giving blood, or it struggles with an elastic band and what appears to be a pill dispenser labelled with the days of the week. Fingers flexing awkwardly, the hand struggles like a dying bug, incapable of any of the maintenance work displayed on the far screen. The effect is poignant, chilling, but never sentimental.

For all its claustrophobic energy, "Semi-detached" is not self-contained. Too much of its power depends on external information: we know the house is a reproduction of Landy's boyhood home because a description of the work mounted on the gallery wall tells us; the same wall-mounted panel which informs us that the DIY images are from a collection owned by Landy's father. While not essential, these facts – let's take them on trust, because this is the Tate and they are displayed behind Perspex – heighten the frisson by confirming what we might otherwise only suspect, that the subject of the piece is the artist's father, whose incapacity is also confirmed by the Perspex panel. It is unfashionable nowadays to expect a work of art in any medium to stand alone; how its content relates to the life of its creator is the stuff of broadsheet profiles. How much easier to consider content's relation to auto-biography than to grapple with matters of technique, consideration of which requires at least a passing knowledge of the art form in question. Everyone, on the other hand, is qualified to gossip. But would any of the undoubted impact of the installation be lost if we were to learn that Landy had faked the biographical element?

Unsurprisingly, the catalogue published to accompany "Semi-detached" moves beyond contextualisation to interpretation; Landy's piece "questions the way in which we value and identify ourselves through labour", the wall-mounted panel says. An essay in the catalogue expounds on this, citing earlier work to further its argument, presumably with Landy's approval. (This includes the infamous 2001 work "Break Down", in which Landy catalogued then systematically destroyed everything he owned, ending, as it happens, with his father's old sheepskin coat.) But then, what an artist sets out to achieve and what the finished article communicates to the rest of us are often two different things, especially if the work is sufficiently complex. If you want to send unambiguous messages, try journalism.

Perhaps the most interesting aspect of "Semi-detached" is its insistence on being taken in passing, a concept that renders my detailed description of the piece all but redundant. Were I not writing this, I would not have stuck around for all three films, approximately one and three-quarter hours of standing or slumping against a wall – in the Duveen Galleries, there are pillars between the seating and the screens, so regarding the work as a cinematic experience is strongly discouraged. Just as well, because there is no narrative here, only grinding repetition, which many experience fleetingly, en route to other rooms. While I was present, people ambled past, wondering who was whistling, or momentarily looked up at the tortured hand, then left wordlessly; a woman in a wheelchair was whizzed through, chatting to her friend about something unconnected to the exhibit; a few spent more time reading the wall-mounted panel than they spent with the work it described; and my 21-month-old daughter charged around, calling me now and then from somewhere out of sight, her voice seamlessly entering the world of the installation to infuse it with a warmth it otherwise lacked.

'SEMI-DETACHED' © MICHAEL LANDY 2004

PHOTO: M. HEATHCOTE & J. FERNANDES

Michael Donaghy 1954–2004

Many of our readers will have been shocked and saddened by the news of Michael Donaghy's death on 16 September, 2004. Here Greta Stoddart, who read a eulogy at Michael's funeral, pays tribute to a man who was a poet, mentor and friend to so very many people.

Those who met Michael will remember his laugh. How quick it came – at our jokes; at his own. Wit and prankster, he found a lightness in everything, and although it was often frivolous, it was also a way of seeing things that was essentially redemptive.

As a poet and teacher Michael was the most subtle and sincere and idiosyncratic of guides. He led us without our knowing to all kinds of knowledge. He showed us a way of looking at the world so that it appeared at once clearer and infinitely more detailed and mysterious.

Given the chance Michael would recite Keats's "Ode to Melancholy"; that beautifully restrained human cry of a poem was like his theme tune. But he wasn't one to wallow. He'd snap things shut with a sudden insight, or witticism. Read his poems and you'll see how the last lines are often the lyrical equivalent of a superbly timed slap in the face – making us sit up, take heed.

Curious, eclectic, insatiable – for Michael it was Keats and James Brown, Marvell and MC Cole; it was the Hayward Gallery and MonkeyWorld, it was Citizen Kane and the 3D Children's Underwater Adventure at IMAX.

He was someone who, for all his teasing and mischief, found an essential humanity in everyone. No one was too unimportant for his time. So people – we – constantly came knocking: for blurbs and favours, for his opinion and praise, for his music and his stories, for him. One of the rare occasions I heard him moan was about how he could never refuse. He talked about getting a T-shirt with the words "When I say YES I really mean NO".

Nearly everything Michael did he did fast. He thought fast and spoke fast, he walked and ate and drank fast. He read fast. When he read his poems, though, he seemed to enter and abide by a completely different sense of time and timing. Perhaps because he knew that it was the poems that really mattered, that it was the poems that needed the proper space and time and that life was somehow a secondary concern, something to be got through – fast.

Fifty years is a bit like the cup half full, the cup half empty. For Michael it was his natural life-span, and though we may mourn the life still to be lived, the poems to be written, we should celebrate the fact that we had him in our midst. The voice we heard in his last book, *Conjure*, often sounded like one speaking out of an absence: which is why it is here, in the poems, that we will ultimately and for ever feel Michael's presence; for it is here, in the poems, that absence has become, finally, a presence, his presence.

A trust fund is in the process of being set up for Michael's son, Ruairi. When available, details will be posted on www.poetrysociety.org.uk, and printed in the next issue of *Poetry News*.

Letters to the Editors

Tessa Jowell's essay is indeed welcome, in its broad principles. And, as your editorial states, her approach needs to be backed by other government ministries, not least the education department.

As the annual debate over the value of A-levels has established, both university tutors and employers have consistently expressed their concerns at the low levels of literacy and numeracy of school leavers.

It is small wonder that many readers have little interest in poetry when they have not even the basic equipment with which to understand its various qualities. And since many contemporary poets and their publishers seem desperate to solicit the interest of such people, and not to make any demands on them for fear of scaring them off, it can scarcely hope to engage the interest of the better educated and intellectually curious, who will find that other artistic media – the novel, serious cinema, classical music, contemporary art – can offer them the sophisticated aesthetic experiences they seek.

The fact, recently highlighted by the "Next Generation" promotion, that 96% of the poetry bought in this country is by dead poets neither surprises nor dismays me. Poetry readers may be fewer in number than those who enjoy rock music or blockbuster films, but they do tend to know quality when they see it, whether in the work of Spenser, Pope, Byron, Dickinson or Pound. An emphasis on this excellence, which can be accessed by anyone, given applied attention and study, is long overdue. It will lead to better readers, and better poets.

Terence Smallwood
Sussex

Jowell's remarks, while breaking with the bean-counting, quota-filling, outreach ethos of her predecessors – art as an instrument of social policy, an approach beloved of Stalinists and Nazis alike – leaves many questions unanswered. In the absence of targets and measurable attainments (which I agree are an anathema to free creativity), how are her various bureaucrats to make their decisions?

To which magazines and publishers will they disburse the meagre percentage of our taxes left over from our military adventures?

While the Treasury seems to give generous guarantees to arms dealers (with the tax payer cheerlessly underwriting sales to dubious nations who have failed to pay up), they are more beady-eyed when it comes to (far more minor) expenditure on the arts. Jowell's policy would rely on independent-minded, fearless, curious, art-loving civil servants and quango-members, highly educated and discriminating yet flexible and open-minded in thought, handing out money to artists whose work may not be appreciated immediately even by critics, academics, and the public, let alone those journalists who wax apoplectic whenever public money is spent on art which they do not understand (nor try to).

What a beautiful world this would be. But I do not think that I will hold my breath.

D. G. Hanson
East Lynne

Thank you for the invitation to consult Tessa Jowell's well-meaning document. It doesn't, though, address a significant problem: that patronage never comes without strings. Artists requiring funding have always had three choices: produce exactly what is demanded by their patrons (whether the State or private individuals and corporations), thus becoming salaried entertainers and courtiers; pretend to please their patrons, and covertly pursue their real agendas (one thinks of the subtlety of poets in Eastern Europe during the Cold War); or go hungry, or worse (there are always some examples of principled artists continuing to produce their own work while denied any institutional help – including some famous figures, who had lamentably painful lives, and are only now posthumously appreciated).

Tessa Jowell, as she points out, is answerable to "the tax payer", that great despotic abstraction. In reality, she is answerable to the media and to her political masters; for her own position is in the gift of a patron too. The same is true of appointees within the arts bureaucracy. They will not be appointed if they are not to the liking of those who allocate the positions.

As your amusing quotation from our poet laureate on the back of your last issue points out, good art is often critical of social reality, not merely reflective of it. Politicians, on the other hand, tend to be shy of criticism, preferring the feel-good aura of "cool Britannia" and so on.

Not that this should worry Britain's poets, who with the exception of a few writers, like Tom Paulin, seem to have little desire to deal with history and politics, and so are unlikely to trouble any politician or bureaucrat, let alone posterity.

Elizabeth Morgan
Cambridge

The *Poetry Review* Crossword No. 5

The sender of the first correct solution opened on 1 December receives a cash prize of £20. Entries should be addressed to *Poetry Review* Crossword, 22 Betterton Street, London WC2H 9BX.

set by ANDRONYMOUS

Solution to the *Poetry Review* Crossword no. 4

Across: 9 Basho, 10 Exact Fare, 11 Simulacra, 12 Homer, 13 Neruda, 14 Cynewulf, 17 The Gawain Poet, 21 Etruscan, 23 Sappho, 25 Dante, 27 Doc Savage, 28 Atomic War, 29 Elide.

Down: 1 Ubi Sunt, 2 Isomorph, 3 Boiled Eggs, 4 Vetch, 5 Paralytic, 6 Itch, 7 Mau-mau, 8 Petrify, 15 Esplanades, 16 Two And Two, 18 Emphasis, 19 Feydeau, 20 Lowered, 22 Renton, 24 Acorn, 26 Evil.

The winner of the *Poetry Review* Crossword no.4 is Susan Woodman. She receives £20.

Across

8 Confused fogey has not quite liberated 22 of poetic type (8)
9 Angry fusilier, running amok, is abandoned (6)
10 "The Birdie Song? Not again!" (Poe) (9)
11 Chilly chat-show host, if familiar (5)
13 Poetic type of 22 puts his heart in a French clog, sends it back (6)
14 Couplet rewritten about one's topical treatment (8)
16 Mocked car still a Daimler inside (4)
17 Class of words without French articles... (5)
18 ...and the rest are horribly late (2,2)
19 Alloy enclosed soft journalist for having a point (8)
20 Nasty malaise, not a poetic 22 (6)
21 At last, our heads are heads of greeting (5)
23 Fats' kind of 22 made of rubber and lye (9)
26 Pelt, bleeding, being washed out and rolled neatly (6)
27 Poke fun at sound wave after a shoe (8)

Down

1 Bed artist given fat fee to dance around like a woman (15)
2 As if a woman artist had meal after throwing up iron loudly (10)
3 In auspicious wise for setter's ascending alone (11)
4 In passing, Yorkshire city (4)
5 Simple: first half of 22 brought up to 1 below 7 (3)
6 20, heartless, can be styled into a flat-topped 22 (4)
7 Steep, rocky 22 after crepuscular month on metal bird (5,4-6)
12 State of sinking island finally replaced with good guy's farming system (11)
14 Beat poet? (5)
15 Luftwaffe film is the upper limit of melancholy (3,4,3)
22 Greeting will rise (4)
24 Log, under magic, becomes primal protagonist of Hughes book (4)
25 Not even peculiar (3)

Editorial
Cheap as chips

The time is past when advertising tried to condition the consumer by the repetition of slogans; today the more subtle forms of publicity represent a whole attitude to life; if you know how to choose you will choose this brand and no other . . . you are being looked after, cared for, told how to live better, in short, how to exist; you are totally and thoroughly programmed, except that you still have to choose between so many good things.

Lefebvre, Everyday Life in the Modern World

Classics are, as [Daisy] Goodwin puts it, as "cheap as chips" to produce, for the simple reason that they are largely out of copyright. If old works could be brought to the front of the shop, then there was money to be made.

Sunday Times, January 26, 2003

It is hard to imagine Wordsworth, had he happened to live in the twenty-first century, settling down to a regular job in an office, although he might have found a berth at Greenpeace. I think this poem is a terrific antidote to the tsunamis of consumer frenzy that overwhelm us all at times.

Daisy Goodwin, Poems to Last a Lifetime

Poets, like other people who work with language, understand that metaphor is not merely ornamental, not merely glitter on an otherwise plain sentence. They know that the metaphors we choose and use say something larger about our attitudes and ideas. They can also conceal truths while ostensibly illuminating them; and they can also reveal truths which their speakers sought to hide.

Take fashion. Like any other form of public speech, fashion tells us something; however inadvertently, it reveals a certain truth. As Matt ffytche's essay on Mallarmé's surprising role as a fashion editor suggests, Mallarmé found in fashion a manifestation of the rootlessness of contemporary culture, a kind of exemplary symptom of modern existence.

Another exemplary symptom of modern existence, with a very different relation to fashion, can be found in bookshops this month: Daisy Goodwin's latest anthology, *Poems to Last A Lifetime*. From the promise of its title to the lifestyle-porn of its jacket design (a soft-focus shot of a vacant sofa and some attractive cushions) to the glossy photos and trendy typefaces within, we have a book which wants to slip in to your life alongside *Nigella Bites* and *The Life-Laundry*. It looks lovely, and it reads easily. It is less a book than an accessory.

All of which would be an inoffensive matter of good business practice, if Goodwin merely printed her simple lyric choices (a lot of Roger McGough, Wendy Cope and Kahlil Gibran, for example, and the briefer love poems of the more demanding writers) and left it at that. Such anthologies are everywhere: no poetry publisher can afford not to move into this market, as Picador's editor has just shown; the financial success can underwrite the rest of their programme, as Bloodaxe discovered with *Staying Alive* (and hopes to repeat with *Being Alive*). Publishers defend these books with vigour, because without them, they would go under.

We are told that it is snobbish and elitist to criticise such books: we are told that anthologies create new readers. The argument is disingenuous. Nothing about these books encourages the general reader to a further engagement with poetry, as sales figures will reflect. And it is perfectly proper for critics to point out the editors' errors and lapses. (Neil Astley's angry response to a few bad reviews for *Staying Alive* never engaged with their actual criticism: that his prose was wretched, his manner anti-intellectual, and some of his selections terrible. He simply accused their authors of being a "bogus cult" intent on spoiling people's fun.)

In Goodwin's case, her prose is shockingly condescending. She writes down to her readers, assuming their ignorance, pretending to be ignorant herself, and traducing her poets in the process. Time and again, poets and poems are reduced to salacious biographical details – the sex lives, the marriages, the illnesses, madnesses and suicides – in prose so cheap and tabloid as to coarsen the poets' own words.

Her responses render each poem as a single, paraphrasable, bite-sized message even as they hypocritically gesture at greater profundity. We are in a world of "dodgy time-shares", "soupy chick-lit dramas", "wife-swapping commuter-belts", "personal theme-songs" and "American *Vogue*", where women want diamonds and chocolates, and fall in love with unsuitable men. This is what people mean by "relevance", presumably.

Glyn Maxwell gets in with a football poem, Edwin Morgan with a cigarette poem, Blake Morrison with a poem about dieting. (Are they pleased?) Robert Graves is love-sick. Byron is a pin-up. Of Mayakovsky we are informed that "after the Revolution he drifted away from politics and devoted himself to poetry", a line shocking in both its falsity and its unstated assumptions. But one suspects that it does not matter whether people read these comments, nor whether they are incorrect. They are ornamental, and serve merely to reassure the reader that Goodwin knows what she is talking about, but is otherwise unthreateningly down to earth.

The effect of the book is to reduce all poetry to simple lyric statements of everyday life. The Auden, Shelley, Byron, Mayakovsky and others who emerge from these pages are characters from glossy magazines, not artists with commitments to language and public life. In fact, it is hard to imagine many of Goodwin's poets appreciating the packaging in which they are being presented. But they are mostly dead, of course, "as cheap as chips"; and there is money to be made, whether from interior decoration, self-help, or Petrarchan sonnets. This is not, as in Mallarmé's case, poetry confronting fashion, but being subsumed by it. There is a difference between selling poetry and selling it out.

*

Editorial note: The editors are delighted that Daljit Nagra's "Look We Have Coming To Dover!", first published in *Poetry Review*, has won the Best Single Poem category of the Forward Prize 2004, and congratulate Daljit on his deserved success.

*

Artist's Note

John Copnall has been widely acknowledged as a serious British painter for nearly 50 years. Winner of the Turner Gold Medal for landscape painting in 1954, he initially achieved acclaim as a figurative artist. From 1955 to 1968 he lived and worked in rural Spain. The wild and rugged terrain was to have a profound effect on his work, eventually inspiring a transition to abstract expressionism. An elected member of the London Group since 1989, John Copnall now lives and works in Bow, East London. His work is characterized by force of colour, a strident approach to brushwork, and a compelling use of collage. These techniques can be interpreted as a response to the jagged skyline which is his backdrop.